Teaching Tomorrow's Leaders Today
Lessons from L.E.A.D.E.R.S.H.I.P. Camp

David Tantillo

PublishAmerica
Baltimore

First printing

At the specific preference of the author, PublishAmerica allowed this work to remain exactly as the author intended, verbatim, without editorial input.

ISBN: 1-4241-3290-8
PUBLISHED BY PUBLISHAMERICA, LLLP
www.publishamerica.com
Baltimore

Printed in the United States of America

"Dave Tantillo has written a business education book in an engaging story format. You find yourself immersed in the characters and competition while at the same time learning leadership fundamentals."
—Jane F. Hoffer, President & CEO of Prescient Applied Intelligence, Inc.

"A creative narrative, which illustrates the development of leadership capacity through collaboration."
—Louis Dash III, D.M.A., Ed.S., Administrator, University Academy College Preparatory Kansas City, Missouri

"Written in the style of The Goal, Teaching Tomorrow's Leaders Today *offers an ideal foundation on leadership for young people in business. This book offers compelling insights in a very accessible and memorable way. The lessons learned from Dave Tantillo's easy story-telling narrative would stick with you. Great leadership is often portrayed as the domain of great heroes. Dave de-mystifies the art of leadership by breaking it down into its component pieces, and brings the individual concepts to life in an entertaining and memorable narrative. Whether you are a new manager or a seasoned executive, this book offers refreshing and powerful insights that you can use to immediately raise your game. The hallmark of a good teacher is someone who can break complex concepts into simple, clear components. In* Teaching Tomorrow's Leaders Today, *Dave Tantillo has cemented his credentials as a great teacher."*
—Alastair Dorward, president & CEO of method

Table of Contents

Foreword

Have you ever asked yourself if you have what it takes to become a leader? Do you have the right experiences? Do you have the best education? Do you physically or emotionally fit the mold? Do you dress like a leader? Will you ever get that title or that position where people will look up to you and admire you for your leadership and the legacy you left behind? If you are asking yourself these kinds of questions, then you have been duped into believing what leadership is all about.

In their article *Seven Lessons for Leading the Voyage to the Future*, James M. Kouzes and Barry Z. Posner, said it best when they claimed "leadership is not the reserve of a few charismatic men and women. It is a process that ordinary people use when they are bringing forth the best from themselves and others." They also state that, "leadership is not a place; it is a process. It involves skills and abilities that are useful whether one is in the executive suite or on the front line, on Wall Street or Main Street."

Teaching Tomorrow's Leaders Today: Lessons from L.E.A.D.E.R.S.H.I.P. Camp is a fictional story about how a human resource representative is asked to interview a potential candidate for a new leadership position in his company. The only problem is that he is not sure what types of questions to ask the candidate because he has forgotten what leadership is all about? As the clock ticks closer to the time of the interview, the human resource representative starts to panic. But, then he remembers several years ago he attended a leadership camp, which taught him ten simple steps in how to become a good leader. Now, can he remember those ten steps in time before his interviewee arrives?

Teaching Tomorrow's Leaders Today: Lessons from L.E.A.D.E.R.S.H.I.P. Camp will teach you ten simple steps you can do today to help you become a good leader tomorrow. This book will also illustrate the fact that leaders are not for a few charismatic men and women. It is free to anyone who wants to embrace it.

Enjoy the journey, as the human resource representative tries to recollect his memories to not only remember the ten steps, but also remember the team of misfits he was part of that summer. Watch how this team of misfits composed of ordinary young adults with physical disabilities, diverse backgrounds, and different personalities make extraordinary things happen on their way to learning the ten steps to becoming a good leader.

Kouzes and Posner said it best, "…whether you are on the front line or in the senior echelon, whether you are a student or a parent, you are capable of developing yourself as a leader far more than tradition has ever assumed possible. When we liberate the leader in everyone, extraordinary things happen."

Leadership is learnable and these ten steps will help you today on your voyage to discover the leader in you tomorrow. Bon Voyage and enjoy the book!

Chapter 1:
New Job Opening

It was 2:00 and the candidate applying for the new position will be here in 30 minutes. Since I was in charge of all the hiring for the company, I had to interview this external candidate who was applying for the Director position of our newly created Leadership Department. The Chairman felt the major problems the company was experiencing is due to the lack of leadership at all levels.

He believed we must start developing and grooming our high potential employees into becoming the leaders of tomorrow immediately. Otherwise, we run the risk of either losing these high potential employees to other companies or suffer the opposite effect…employee burn out! Either case could make the company's bottom line look bleak in the short term and non-existent in the long term.

Since our Training and Development Department did not have the expertise to lead this initiative, the Chairman had to act fast and create a new position and department. Fortunately, he heard from some of his colleagues about an individual who led some major initiatives for their employer who was struggling to survive. This person miraculously turned the company around and was touted by Wall Street as one of the "Up-and-Coming Leaders" of the future. So, the Chairman made some phone calls and convinced this person to apply for the position.

At first glance, the candidate's resume looked to be average. He graduated high honors with an MBA, but it was only from a local college. He only held middle management positions with his current employer, and the company was rather small according to Wall Street standards. He did however cite many accomplishments and awards he had received inside and outside of work with regards to being a good leader.

Then, it hit me! What did I know about leadership? I work for a company who doesn't teach leadership. I'm not in a leadership position. I probably don't even have the qualities to be a leader. How do I interview a potential candidate for a leadership position, when I myself wouldn't know a leader if I walked into one?

I had to come up with some thought provoking questions about leadership quickly, but I didn't know where to begin. I guess not ever being a leader doesn't totally disqualify me from knowing about leadership. I only need to know what it takes or at least identify the qualities that make a leader.

I started scanning my office to see if there was anything in the room that could help me start listing leadership qualities or at least identify some steps people follow that make them great leaders. It was then I noticed a particular framed picture on one of my shelves.

It was the picture of *"Team L.O.T."* from the Leadership Camp I attended when I was fourteen. *"Team L.O.T."* was my first and best experience I ever had working with other people who all worked together and managed to pull off one of the most lopsided victories in Leadership Camp history.

That's it! Leadership Camp! I remember now. I had learned what leadership was all about that summer. Now, if I could just remember what I learned long ago. I took out a pad of paper and a pen and looked at my watch. Only twenty minutes to go before the interview. I better start thinking hard and writing fast. Now, what happened that first day at camp…

Chapter 2:
Look Fear in the Face

"We gain strength, and courage, and confidence by each experience in which we really stop to look fear in the face…we must do that which we think we cannot." (Eleanor Roosevelt)

It was the first day of summer vacation and my parents took no time at all to register me for my first camp. It was called Leadership Camp and it was going to last two whole weeks. I wasn't too happy with my parents because camp was supposed to be fun—not learning junky stuff like leadership. They dropped me off 9 A.M. in front of the local high school, which I will be starting this Fall as a Freshman. I saw nineteen other poor kids who were going to suffer the same fate as I. There is nothing worse than having to learn, when it's my vacation time.

All of us stood in the parking lot until a rather odd looking man came out of the main office to greet us. He didn't look much like a leader. Maybe he's going to tell us that camp was cancelled because the Camp Leader found a group of adults who cared more about being a leader than a bunch of teenage kids who just want to have fun during their summer break.

That thought came to a drastic halt when the first words that came out of his mouth were, "Please follow me."

Just like the Pied Piper, all twenty of us followed this man into the high school where he brought us to the school library.

The second sentence that came out of his mouth was, "Please sit down."

As I sat down, I thought to myself at that very moment that we were dealing with either a former drill sergeant from the armed forces or someone who loves picking on young kids. All of a sudden this man started to speak to us in more than three word sentences.

"Why did you all follow me and then sit down when I told you too?"

One of the kids spoke up, and said, "Cause you told us too!"

The man spoke again, saying, "Do you guys even know who I am?"

Another kid spoke, saying, "You're our Leadership Camp Leader. Right?"

The man replied, yet again, "What makes you think I am your Camp Leader?"

Then, out of nowhere, I heard a girl's voice say, "Please don't think I am rude sir, but you are either telling us what to do using three word sentences or asking us questions without answering the most important question for us. Are you our Camp Leader for Leadership Camp or not?"

Every kid's head turned to this voice, and there sat the prettiest young girl I had ever seen. She was a skinny, little girl with wavy, black hair that bounced off her shoulders when she talked. Her eyes were between hazel and green. She was dressed more like she was ready to go out to dinner, rather than playing at a summer camp. For a small, petite girl, she sure had some broad shoulders to give a reply like that to the drill sergeant.

"Finally, someone has the courage to stand up and ask an intelligent question," the man replied. He continued, by saying, "Yes, I am your Camp Leader and my name is Dr. Bermat, but you can call me Dr. B. I started asking all of you questions at first because I wanted to show all of you what leadership is not. With a show of hands, did all of you believe I was going to be your Camp Leader because I am an adult?" All twenty kids raised their hands in total agreement.

"A good leader has the ability to have people follow them without saying a word or in my case…just three word sentences," he said with a chuckle. Everyone turned to the pretty young girl who originally made that comment. Dr. B. too looked at the young girl and kindly asked, "May I ask your name please?"

The young girl replied in a guarded tone, "My name is Jill."

Dr. B. responded to Jill by saying, "Well, I haven't even begun my speech yet about how all of you will learn the ten steps to becoming a good leader and you managed to already exhibit the first step, which I coined *Look*."

Jill became embarrassed; however, as Dr. B. began to speak, I could tell that she was feeling mighty proud she naturally stumbled upon the first step in being a good leader. She started to sit upright and listened to every word that proceeded from his mouth with regards to what we will be learning while at Leadership Camp. Dr. B. began explaining what the word *Look* has to do with being a good leader.

"*Look* is short for *Look Fear in the Face*. What I mean by looking fear in the face is that good leaders can see the future and start to look for a solution to a problem, when they can come to grips with their own fear and reality. Good leaders build character, confidence, and courage when they can conquer their own fear by staring it right in the face. Why do you think Christopher Columbus was a good leader? He overcame his fear that the world was not flat. He stopped letting his fear dictate how to explore the new world and eventually discovered America," Dr.B. said.

Dr. B. then turned to Jill, and said proudly, "Jill, it took a lot of courage to *Look* me straight in the face, and say what you said to me. I would bet not too many young adults would ever do that nowadays. Great job, and I look forward to you learning the next nine steps."

With that, Dr. B. went into explaining to us what Leadership Camp was all about. He told us that the ultimate goal of camp was for him to teach tomorrow's leaders today, which by the way is the slogan for the camp. He went on to inform us that we are those tomorrow's leaders, and he will teach us over the next two weeks how to become those leaders of tomorrow.

Next, Dr. B. went into his speech about how Leadership Camp will be run for the next two weeks. All twenty of us would break into two groups. We would learn one step each day by performing some sort of competitive team activity. Each step would build on the previous step until we would learn all ten steps. Each team would select a leader each day for every event. No one on the team could be the leader more than once. Finally, he said at the end of the two weeks, one individual, who has learned and performed all the steps of becoming a good leader, will receive the *Young Leader of Tomorrow Award.*

He said, we had the rest of the day to meet, talk with each other, and display our personal profiles (a prerequisite for Leadership Camp) on the table next to the chalkboard. At 3:00, Dr. B. said he would return and help us pick both teams, so we could know our team prior to going into Tuesday's first competitive team activity. With that, Dr. B. exited the library and everyone started to mingle with one another.

As promised, Dr. B. showed up at 3:00 sharp.

"O.K. everyone please be seated. We need to pick teams, and we need to select two leaders from among you to start us off. I will first ask if there are any volunteers. If no one volunteers, then I will choose the leaders to start," Dr. B. said. As suspected, no one volunteered.

"You leave me no choice since you all are afraid to stand up," he exclaimed with disappointment.

All of a sudden, Jill stood up, and courageously said, "I will *Look Fear in the Face* and be the first team leader."

"Good answer, Jill," Dr. B. replied. "Apparently someone learned something from this morning."

After Jill stood up and was praised, everyone else raised their hand, so they could be the next team leader. Dr. B. told everyone else to think of a number from 1 to 100. The person coming closest to the number he was thinking would be the next team leader.

As a result, Alex came the closest to Dr. B.'s number. How appropriate! Alex was one of the most popular kids who had it all: good looks, good physique, very strong, very athletic, and very confident in himself. Dr. B. explained to Jill and Alex that both of them could pick in whatever boy-girl sequence they liked, as long as their team had five girls and five boys in the end. Not to brag, but Jill picked me second!

Here is how the teams stacked up:

Jill's Team:	Alex's Team:
Dave	Jackson
Jaden	Adam
Chris	Logan
Jacob	Trevor
Emily	Destiny
Grace	Brooke
Isabella	Angelina
Olivia	Jessica
Ben	Brittany

There was only one big problem I saw when the picking was done. Alex's team looked like a bunch of athletes, who could model for a fitness magazine. Jill's team looked like a bunch of nerds, who could model for a misfit magazine. I'm not sure what Jill was thinking when she picked our team, but I trusted her instincts because she could *Look Fear in the Face.*

I had only one question on my mind. Was she prepared to *Look* embarrassed and *Face* humiliation when Alex's Team beats us in every team activity? I guess with all things considered, I get to be embarrassed and humiliated with the prettiest girl in Leadership Camp. Plus, also she picked me second!

As Dr. B. was walking away, he said he wanted all of us to be in the school gymnasium at 9 A.M. sharp to start our first competitive team activity. He wanted us to be prepared and dressed to play an indoor athletic activity. Plus, he wanted us to come up with a team name that truly represented our team. Finally, he gave us a hint of what we would be doing and learning tomorrow.

Dr. B. said, "You can't hit what you can't see. Sometimes to *Look* is not enough. Have a great day. I will see you all tomorrow to learn step two in becoming a good leader."

Chapter Summary

- Step 1 in becoming a leader is the ability to "*Look Fear in the Face.*"
- Good leaders can see the future and start to look for a solution to a problem, when they can come to grips with their own fear and reality.
- Leaders build character, confidence, and courage when they can conquer their own fear by staring it right in the face.
- Leaders have the ability to have people follow them without even saying a word.

Chapter 3:
Envision the Vision

"A man to carry on a successful business must have imagination. He must see things as in a vision, a dream of the whole thing." (Charles Schwab—Founder, Chairman and CEO of Charles Schwab Company)

As I walked into the school gymnasium at 8:50 A.M. on Tuesday, I noticed two apparent things. First, if you thought my team looked pathetic in our normal street attire, you should have seen us in our gym clothes. Our team boasted a group of young adults ranging from overweight to paper thin, abnormally tall to munchkin size, and uncoordinated to the physically disabled. Second, as suspected yesterday, Alex's team boasted young men who could model for any muscle magazine, while the young girls could model for any beauty magazine. This was going to be a long and agonizing day! All of a sudden, I heard my name being called from the far corner of the gym.

"Dave, over here," Jill shouted. She was waving me over to talk with her.

"Hey Jill! What's up?" I said happily.

Jill replied, "I am so glad you came over. I wanted your opinion on the name for our team. I shared it with the other people on the team. They thought it was great. What do you think about the name *Team L.O.T.?*"

I was not totally disappointed by the name, but I had to ask the question. "Why *Team L.O.T.?*" Jill sensed that I was not too thrilled about the name, but she gracefully explained the name without being defensive.

"The word L.O.T. means Leaders of Tomorrow. We could call our team the *Leaders of Tomorrow,*" Jill said in a bubbly tone.

It did have a nice ring to it. I gave her my thumbs up, and we headed towards the other members of our team.

At 9:00 sharp again, Dr. B. came clamoring through the gym doors with his velour purple gym outfit. I think his clothes were stuck in a time warp, but I didn't want to say anything.

"O.K. everyone. Please have a seat on the bleachers. We have a few things we have to go over before we begin today's competitive activity," replied Dr. B.

He continued, by saying, "First things first. I need both of your team names and why you picked them. Jill you can go first."

Jill stood up proudly, and said, "Our team name will be *Team L.O.T.,* which stands for *Leaders of Tomorrow.*" That very moment, an explosion of laughter came from Alex's team.

"You have to be kidding me. That name is so lame," scoffed Alex.

Dr. B. immediately stopped him, and replied, "Alright Alex. What is the name of your team?"

Alex tilted his head high along with the others, and exclaimed, "We will call ourselves *Team Delta Force!*"

Dr. B. of course had to ask the inevitable, "And, why the name *Team Delta Force,* Alex?" "*Team* because we are a team obviously. *Delta* because it means *change* in Greek. *Force* because we are a force to be reckoned with. Put it all together. We are the *team* who is going to inflict so much *force* on the other team they will *change* their minds about why they signed up for Leadership Camp in the first place," Alex exclaimed with his cocky and confident attitude.

As Dr. B. was trying not to laugh, I could sense everyone on our team except for Jill was a little bit nervous about completing the rest of Leadership Camp. No one wanted to be physically hurt and humiliated by the other team.

"Very clever Alex in coming up with your name, but it takes more than a fancy name, physical force, and intimidation to become a leader. Let your actions guide you, and not your words. Speaking of actions, we have our first competitive activity to help you identify and learn the second step in becoming a good leader," said Dr. B.

He continued, by saying, "I want everyone to play volleyball all morning long. Rotate players in, so everyone can play. After lunch, I will have both teams play a match (best of three games). I will see everyone at 1:00 sharp. Have fun practicing." Dr. B turned, and exited out of the gym doors.

Both teams felt a little awkward after he left, but that soon passed when Alex's Team turned to our team and said "Let's start practicing even though it's not gonna help you much this afternoon!" Each team took a side.

Jill was about to serve, when she calmly and coolly said to Alex, "Let me give you a piece of advice. It is better to be thought of as being stupid, than to open your mouth and be known as stupid."

Alex didn't understand Jill's advice, so he replied the only way he could, "Oh shut-up, and serve the ball."

It was 1:00, and Dr. B. strutted in with his Saturday Night Fever velour-jogging suit again, but this time he had a huge white sheet with him folded up.

"Good afternoon everyone. I hope you practiced well because it's probably not going to help you this afternoon. I forgot to mention that it's not just volleyball you will be playing. It will be midnight volleyball," he said with a secretive grin on his face.

With that, Dr. B. threw this huge white sheet over the net. It covered the entire net from left to right and from the top of the net to the bottom of the floor.

Alex immediately asked, "What's up Dr. B.? How are we going to see the ball?"

Dr. B. replied, "It's all about step two in becoming a good leader. When the match is over, hopefully you will understand why I used the sheet. So, who will be the team leader for each team for this activity?"

Alex's team huddled together, and then a minute later they all replied in unison, "Brittany!" They selected her because she is the captain of her varsity high school volleyball team. Our team huddled and we all looked at each other in a daze.

"I think Ben should be our team leader," Jill said with a confident smile. Everyone but Ben raised a hand in agreement immediately

19

because none of us wanted to be the first team leader to lose.

Ben might be a good choice I thought, but he was the silent type. He seemed to have all the physical abilities to lead us in volleyball. He stood well over six feet tall, and had very large hands for a kid his age. The only problem I thought is that he is hearing impaired. How would he communicate, or lead us if he could barely talk to us or hear us?

Knowing Jill, she must see something the rest of us couldn't see. In any event, Ben was our leader, and we were all about to get embarrassed en route to learning the second step of what it takes to become a good leader. I bet the second step is humility or handling defeat gracefully.

Team Delta Force won the coin toss and elected to serve the first game. As predicted, when the final whistle blew at the end of the first game, *Team Delta Force* beat us fifteen to nothing. We all looked at Ben for some guidance, but he looked a little perplexed as to why we played so badly.

Ben put his hand on his chin, and he began thinking. He seemed like he was in some sort of trance for a few seconds. Then, Ben tapped his head as though he had an idea. He rearranged all of us, and put us in a different rotation. Personally, I didn't think any changes would help. We didn't even score one point in the last game!

Even though we served first in the second game, *Team Delta Force* came out of the gates with an early lead. When we finally scored our first point, everyone was jumping for joy, but Ben. He seemed to be perplexed again as to how we scored the point. I was just happy we scored a point! The game continued on, but then as I predicted, *Team Delta Force* was now serving game and match point.

All of a sudden, Ben signaled Dr. B. for a time out. I looked up at the scoreboard, and the score read fourteen to eight in favor of *Team Delta Force*. I bet Ben is getting us together to say even if we lose, we tried our best and scored eight points on them. Ben could speak a little because he was not born deaf. He told us not to panic because he figured out how to win the game. He asked us to trust him, and to do exactly what he said.

Struggling to pronounce his words, Ben replied, "Now, and until the end of the game, I want everyone to play back when we are receiving the ball. When we are on the attack, do not pass the ball deep. Just dink or dump it softly over the net."

We all looked at each other in bewilderment, but Ben was confident when he spoke to us. It was as though he saw something we couldn't see. I don't know what he was seeing because there was a huge white net in front of us!

To our amazement, Ben was right in his advice. After the timeout, we were able to mount a comeback. We won the game in sudden death sixteen to fourteen. We scored eight consecutive points! The teams were tied one game a piece with the third and final game yet to start. Since they won the coin toss, *Team Delta Force* again got to serve first. We were starting to feel a little confident, but we were not sure if our win was pure luck or a product of good scheming. Ben again approached us with more advice for the final game.

"O.K. Let's start pushing the ball deep into their corners now. I think they'll start cheating up because we started dumping the ball close to the net at the end of the last game," Ben said.

We all shook our heads in agreement because it sounded logical. I honestly thought to myself that we might have a good chance to really win the game and match. Everything was going as Ben predicted. We came out with a strong lead and the score was now ten to two in our favor.

Then, something really strange happened. Little by little, *Team Delta Force* started chipping away at our lead until the score was now tied at ten all. Ben immediately called a timeout and we huddled together.

"I think they've caught onto our game plan," Ben said.

He continued, by saying "I have an idea, but it will require everyone working together and focusing on my left hand." We all looked at each other like Ben was talking crazy.

"I'll explain later, but I want everyone to listen closely. When we're about to pass the ball over the net, please look at the number of fingers I'll be showing you with my left hand. If I hold up one finger, push the ball deep into the corner. If I hold up two fingers, then push the ball in the center of the court. And, if I hold up three fingers, then dump the ball gently over the net. You need to trust me on this," Ben said.

Ben's advice paid off! Within ten minutes, we not only won the third game and obviously the match, but we won the first competitive team activity.

"Well done *Team L.O.T.*," Dr. B. shouted proudly. "You've won the first competitive event. First things first. What did you do different to win the last game? It looked like you lost momentum when the score became tied."

We all pointed to Ben, and cheered in unison, "It was all Ben!" Ben's face immediately turned red and he started looking at the gym floor shyly.

Dr. B. walked over to Ben and asked him in a soothing way, "Ben, share with everyone what you did to help your team win."

Ben hesitated a moment. He didn't like to talk to large crowds because his speech was slurred due to his disability, but this time he decided to speak. I guess he was so proud of the accomplishment his pride made his fear melt away.

"In the beginning, I knew my team was intimidated by the white sheet over the net. It blinded us from seeing the other team. I couldn't see through the net, but I could envision what could be happening because I did see a ball being passed around in the air above the net. So, I studied how the ball was spinning and the direction it was going all the time when the other team was passing the ball around. I realized they were playing back the whole time during the first and second game, so I called a timeout in the second game. I told my team to start dumping the ball. We won the second game of the match because the other team did not adjust to our new strategy," Ben said with a proud smile.

Ben continued, by saying, "However, it didn't take long for *Team Delta Force* to realize what we were up to, and that is why they stole our momentum away from us temporarily and tied up the score in game three. I called a timeout because we wanted to stop their momentum, but I had to think quickly to come up with a new plan.

Then it hit me! We've spent all this time trying to look through the net when we could've just looked around the net. After the ball is in play, I peered around the net and looked how the other team was positioned to return our volley. I then told my team with a show of fingers where to hit the ball when it was our turn to return the volley. We basically hit it to where they weren't. That's how we won."

Alex was enraged and screamed, "They cheated, and we should be awarded the victory."

Dr. B. immediately stopped Alex dead in his tracks, by saying, "A good leader would listen first before passing judgment!" Alex instantaneously shut up, but I could tell he was not happy.

Dr. B. continued, by saying, "Ben did what any good leader would do. First, he understood all the rules and figured out a way to use the rules to his advantage. Let me explain. When the ball is volleying, a player can walk or run outside of their playing area as long as they do not cross the centerline, which does extend beyond the playing court. I observed Ben stepping out of the playing area legally, but I didn't know at the time what he was up to. Now it makes sense what he was trying to do, which brings us to the second behavior.

When you cannot see the answer to a problem, you have three options. The first option is to give up. This is not an option for a good leader by the way. The second option is to apply the principle of Diversity. Use another pair of eyes to look for you. Ask your family, your friends, your colleagues, your employees, or even a complete stranger. Diversity is not about skin color. It is about Diversity of thought and in this case Diversity of eyesight or point of view.

The third option is what Ben did. If you don't have the time or option to ask another person, then change your vantage point. Let me ask all of you a question. What would you do if the sun was blinding you while you were playing outfield in a softball game?"

Everyone one was quiet at first, but then Alex jokingly said, "I would wear some sunglasses!"

"Excellent Alex," said Dr. B.

He went on, saying, "I didn't think of that one, but a good answer. Sunglasses provide us with another lens or vantage point to help us find a solution. Anyone else think they would do something different?"

Ben replied by saying, "I guess I would turn my head and body slightly to shield some of the sunlight."

"Right on!" Dr. B. said with excitement. "You changed your vantage point so you can see the batter better. This brings us to step two in becoming a good leader. The ability to *'Envision the vision.'* A good leader must *envision* where he wants to go and be in the future. He needs to view patterns or study trends that are occurring in the marketplace. Sometimes obstacles prevent him to *'Envision the vision.'* Instead of cursing the darkness because you cannot see your vision, light a candle.

You can light a candle by *'balconizing'* your vantage point. If you want to see the big picture without obstacles in your way, go to the balcony or some high point of reference. It is there where you can *'Envision the vision.'* Ben's balcony was when he stepped out of the playing area to see his solution (i.e. how *Team Delta Force* were positioning themselves). It was at that point Ben *Envisioned* what had to be done to win the game. Well done, Ben," Dr. B. said.

All of a sudden our team burst into cheers, and praised Ben for leading us to victory.

I turned to Jill, and said, "You did it again. You suggested Ben to lead us, and he came through in the clutch!"

Dr. B. interrupted our small celebration and replied, "Alright. We've learned the first two steps in becoming a good leader. Step three will be tomorrow. Here is a hint as to what you'll be learning, and what your activity will be. If you're not united in what you do, obstacles will throw you off course and prevent you from winning the race. Good luck. I will see you tomorrow at 9 A.M. sharp at the track and field stadium. Please wear something appropriate for an outdoor activity." With that, Dr. B. turned and walked out of the gym.

Chapter Summary

- Step 2 in becoming a leader is the ability to *"Envision the Vision."*
- A good leader must *envision* where he wants to be in the future. He needs to view patterns or study trends that are occurring in the marketplace.

- When you cannot see the answer to a problem, you have two options:
    1.)   Apply the principle of Diversity. Use another pair of eyes to look for you. Ask your family, your friends, your colleagues, your employees, or even a complete stranger.
    2.)   If you don't have the time or option to ask another person, then change your vantage point.
- A good leader would first understand all the rules and then figure out a way to use the rules to his advantage.
- Let your actions guide you and not your words.
- Instead of cursing the darkness because you cannot see your vision, light a candle.
- You can light a candle by *"balconizing"'* your vantage point. If you want to see the big picture without obstacles in your way, go to the balcony or some high point of reference. It is there where you can *"Envision the Vision."*

Chapter 4:
Assemble the Team

"It's not just about assembling a team—that's nothing new. The main point is to first get the right people on the bus (and the wrong people off the bus) before you figure out where to drive it." (Jim Collins—author of *Good to Great*.)

It had rained all Tuesday night, so the field in the stadium was quite muddy and slippery Wednesday morning. As predicted, Dr. B. walked onto the field at 9:00 A.M. This time he was sporting a turquoise velour gym suit. I wished somebody would tell him his choice of colors and style of clothing really wasn't flattering, but I figured if he was happy that's all that counted. Dr. B. began speaking as he came closer to both teams.

"Did anyone figure out the competitive activity or the third step in becoming a good leader?"

There was dead silence, until Grace on our team said, "I don't know about the third step, but I think we will we be running in an obstacle course? I'm just guessing because you used the word obstacle and the word course in your hint yesterday."

Dr. B. said with a smile, "Very impressive, Grace!"

Dr. B. continued, "Yes. Both teams need to run a ten-stage obstacle course. The team whose member completes the tenth stage first wins the event. Once again, I need you to pick a team leader. It's the team leader's responsibility to assign a member to each stage of the course. I'll give you ten minutes to perform both tasks."

Feeling confident about winning yesterday, Ben spoke, by saying

"Grace, how about you being our team leader? You figured out the hint Dr. B. gave us yesterday."

As predicted, everyone immediately raised his or her hands in agreement. Feeling pressured, Grace "gracefully" accepted the nomination.

"I'll be the team leader, but I have no idea who should do what stage," she said with concern.

"I'll help you Grace," Jill said with confidence.

"Thank you so much Jill," Grace said as though the weight of the world was lifted off her shoulders.

They both stepped away from the team to discuss the game plan for the team. A few minutes went by. Grace and Jill returned with smiles on their faces.

"O.K. everyone, you selected me as your team leader, so please trust that there is a reason why I picked certain members to perform certain stages of the obstacle course. I'll explain later why I chose each of you for the particular stage you will do," Grace said firmly.

At that moment, Grace rattled off each member's name and each stage he/she would do. Grace selected me to do the rock wall stage. I've never climbed one before, so I don't have any idea why she picked me to do that stage. Suddenly, Dr. B. chimed in, so I didn't have time to ask Grace why she picked me for that particular stage.

"O.K. teams, I need a team leader, and I need a list of what members of your team will be competing in each stage."

"I'll be the team leader for *Team Delta Force*," Jessica blurted out with an attitude.

She continued her arrogance, by saying, "We'll win this event because *Team L.O.T.* won't be able to go around their biggest obstacle."

"What obstacle is that?" Grace said curiously.

"Your heads! They're so big from winning the last event that you'll keep falling over your two feet. You'll be top heavy," Jessica replied sarcastically.

Dr. B. replied to Jessica, by saying, "We'll see if it's cockiness or confidence you are referring too when the tenth person crosses the finish line first. *Team L.O.T.*, who'll be your leader?"

Now hesitant after Jessica's remark, Grace replied, "I guess I'm the team leader for *Team L.O.T.*"

"You guess, or are you the team leader?" Dr. B. asked. Grace turned to our team, and we all nodded to her giving our reassurance that we wanted her as our team leader.

She replied this time confidently saying, "I'm the team leader. And by the way Jessica, we weren't lucky yesterday."

Dr. B. jumped in, and said, "Everyone go to your particular stage and practice all morning. I'll be back at 1:00 to start the competition. See you after lunch." With that, Dr. B. walked off the field, and we all went to our respective stages to practice.

When we had just finished lunch, we looked up, and saw Dr. B. standing there with his turquoise velour gym suit with a smile on his face.

"It's 1:00. It's time to start the competition, and to learn step three of how to become a good leader," Dr. B. said.

He continued, by saying, "Everyone take your place in your respective stage. When I blow my whistle, the person in stage one will have to complete his or her stage first before the next member of the team can start the next stage. We'll progress through each stage in numerical order from one to ten. The team member who completes the tenth stage first will win the event for his or her team. Are you ready? Get set. Go!"

Immediately *Team Delta Force* came out with a vengeance, and was completing each stage faster than our team and had about a thirty second lead over us. They kept the lead going into the tenth stage. It all came down to Jessica from *Team Delta Force,* and Grace from our team competing in the tenth stage.

The tenth stage involved starting a campfire by rubbing two sticks together. Once they get the fire going, the team member had to build a fire up high enough to light an unlit torch positioned above the campfire area. Once lit, the team member will pick up the torch, and run across the finish line.

With a thirty second lead, Jessica from *Team Delta Force* started the tenth stage like a woman on a mission. She started throwing all these sticks and logs into the campfire area and started right away furiously rubbing two sticks together.

When Jacob from *Team L.O.T.* finished the ninth stage, Grace went right to work. The only problem was that Grace seemed as though she had given up already when she started the tenth stage. She was very slow and methodical in all her movements. She was slower than a turtle stuck in gum!

Now Grace was not the most athletic person in the world. She was a short, homely, girl with brown hair and braces. She was skinny as a rail and wore glasses that had lenses as thick as a pancake. She started to build the campfire by gently laying leaves first, properly laying little twigs next, and then leaned logs against each other above the leaves and twigs to make the campfire look like an Indian teepee.

Grace didn't even flinch when we all noticed smoke coming from Jessica's campfire. Then, Grace did the most bizarre thing! Instead of rubbing two sticks together, Grace took off her glasses and held them above the leaves in the campfire.

"What are you doing?" screamed everybody on our team. She didn't move a muscle or even pay attention to us. Jessica's campfire was now showing some flames. But, wait a minute. Grace's campfire was now smoking. It took Grace only thirty seconds to start the fire by holding a pair of glasses. It took Jessica all her strength to start her fire, which by the way took three minutes. Just when we thought we were going to win, Jessica's fire started to burn bigger and higher.

We were all screaming, "Hurry up, Grace. Hurry up!"

She turned to us, and said with her homely voice, "Just be patient, and watch Jessica's campfire."

We all looked at each other, and couldn't figure out why she wanted us to watch Jessica's campfire instead of hers. So, we did as she asked. We watched Jessica jump for joy one minute, and then scream at the top of her lungs the next minute. Her huge fire started to dwindle until there was no more flame. She was franticly trying to rekindle the fire, but it was too late. Not because she couldn't start it up again, but because

29

Grace was already walking across the finish line with her torch. We were all in shock. Even *Team Delta Force* couldn't believe this scrawny little girl with Coke® bottle glasses just beat them without a bead of sweat on her face.

"Well done, *Team L.O.T.* And, well done, Grace," Dr. B. said with a grin on his face.

"I can't wait to hear how you guys pulled this one off," Alex said with a bitter tone.

Dr. B. stopped Alex in his tracks, and replied, "Alex, you never heard of the phrase 'Grace under pressure?' I believe that saying must have been referring to our little Grace on *Team L.O.T.* She was an inspiration without perspiration and desperation! Grace, you must tell us how you pulled this victory off."

Adjusting her thick glasses on her nose, Grace replied, "At first, I didn't know who should do what stage. Better yet, I didn't know what stage I could do because I don't have many talents. It was Jill's suggestion that sparked my idea. She told me to assign everyone a stage according to his or her talents or skills. I told her that I didn't know everyone's talents or skills. She told me I did know, but I didn't realize it.

She said she noticed that I had read all the personal profiles of everyone on our team. You know the profiles we handed to you on the first day. You said we could read them if we wanted, so we could get to know each other a little deeper and maybe help us strike up casual conversations. Well, I *Looked fear in the face* and I *Envisioned* what I had to do. Since I have a photographic memory, I matched each of my teammates to each stage based on what they like to do in their spare time."

Grace continued, by saying, "Jill likes to go to the beach and play in the water, so she did the swimming stage. Dave loves to climb trees, so I had him climb the rock wall stage. Chris loves to shoot things with his pellet gun, so I had him do the archery stage. Logan loves to jog for exercise, so I had him do the running stage. I am sure you are getting the picture by now.

Lastly, I decided to do the campfire stage. Not because I love to light fires, but because I was a girl scout for a few years. They taught us how to build fires by rubbing sticks, using flint, and using a magnifying glass. Or, in my situation, I used my thick Coke® bottle glasses. The only reason Jessica didn't win was because she didn't know how to properly build a fire.

You always start with leaves, then twigs, and then larger logs. She skipped the twigs! Her flames were high and strong in the beginning, but that came to an abrupt end when all her leaves burned up and there were no twigs to keep the fire burning. I stacked all the right forms of kindling in the right order and the result was a blazing campfire. I guess I was lucky putting all my teammates in the right position because the end result was a win. It's all elementary if you really stop and think about it."

"Way to go, Grace!" Dr. B. shouted.

He continued, by saying, "You just paraphrased the third step of becoming a good leader…*Assemble*! It's not enough to just have a team of highly qualified and motivated people. If the right person is not in the right place, then you are headed for failure.

For example, if you were the coach of a football team and you had the best quarterback in the league and center in the league, chances are you are going to win many games and perhaps a championship or two down the road. What happens if you told the quarterback to start playing center and the center to start playing quarterback this season? The result would be disastrous and a losing season would be inevitable.

Assembling a team means being able to perform all five of the following steps. First, you have to know what it takes to perform each job or task properly the first time. Second, you have to know all the skills, knowledge, and abilities of all the members on your team. Third, leverage your people's strengths by matching their skill sets to those jobs requiring their respective skill sets.

Fourth, if a team member continues to stumble in their assigned job or task, then reassign them to another job or task that compliments their skill sets. Finally, if the team member fails in their reassignment, then its time to part ways with that team member. Just like in football, if you cannot perform well at your position or cannot contribute in any other way, then you get released. It gives the team an opportunity to move forward with their plans and the released player an opportunity to be picked up by another team, who might need his skill sets."

"Wow! I did that. I assembled a team without even realizing it," said Grace in amazement.

Dr. B. responded with, "Yes you did, but assembling a team is still not enough to become a good leader. Kick this around in your head after you leave today. Putting the right people in the right places is no good unless they know how to do the right thing at the right time. This is your hint for tomorrow with regards to what you'll be learning next and what game you'll be playing tomorrow. Good luck. I will see you tomorrow at 9 A.M. sharp on the baseball field."

Chapter Summary

- Step 3 in becoming a leader is the ability to *"Assemble the Team."*
- It's not enough to just have a team of highly qualified and motivated people. If the right person is not in the right place, then you are headed for failure.
- Assembling a team means being able to perform all five of the following steps:

  1.) Know what it takes to perform each job or task properly the first time.

  2.) Know all the skills, knowledge, and abilities of all the members on your team.

  3.) Leverage your people's strengths by matching their skill sets to those jobs requiring their respective skill sets.

  4.) If a team member continues to stumble in their assigned job or task, then reassign them to another job or task that compliments their skill sets.

  5.) If the team member fails in their reassignment, then its time to part ways with that team member.

Chapter 5
Discuss the Vision

"Leadership is not magnetic personality—that can just as well be a glib tongue. It is not making friends and influencing people—that is flattery. Leadership is lifting a person's vision to higher sights, the raising of a person's performance to a higher standard, the building of a personality beyond its normal limitations." (Peter F. Drucker)

As predicted, Dr. B. showed up at 9 A.M. on the dot. He walked onto the baseball field wearing…Yep! You guessed right. He was sporting another velour gym suite. This time it was canary yellow. There must have been a sale at the local thrift store. Dr. B. must have picked up all the available colors in his size. Anyway, it was day four and we were going to learn the next step in becoming a good leader. We just didn't know what we had to do this time to learn it.

"O.K. everyone please gather around home plate," said Dr. B.

He continued, by saying, "Many of you are probably guessing we're going to play either hardball or softball, since we're on a baseball diamond. If you guessed that, then you've guessed wrong. We'll be playing kickball today. Once again, I will leave you to practice all morning. Upon my return at 1:00, I will need the name of your team leader. Any questions?" Dr. B. waited a moment, but no one had a question. With that, he turned around and marched off the playing field.

We huddled up on our side of the field and began our typical morning ritual of forcing members into being the next team leader. We would nominate someone and everyone else raised his/her hand quickly to prevent disagreement. However, this time something different happened. Someone actually volunteered before we started the nomination process.

"I would like to be the next team leader if that's O.K. with everyone," said Jaden with some hesitancy in his voice. He wasn't sure how everyone would react since this was a break away from our normal gutless ways.

"I second your nomination and I am proud of you for standing up Jaden," Jill said confidently!

I jumped into the mix and said, "All in favor of Jaden being our next team leader please raise your hand." Everyone raised their hands so fast in the air they could've caught a fly passing by. I had to ask Jaden about his sudden urge to lead our team.

"Excuse the pun, but why are you stepping up to the plate to be our leader on this event?" I asked curiously. His response was quite admirable and inspiring.

"After watching Jill, Grace, and Ben step up and deliver for the team, I felt that I needed to step up and also deliver. I feel I can contribute heavily on this event, and could possibly lead our team to another victory," Jaden stated confidently.

"Good enough for me, so what do you want us to do?" I asked Jaden. He told us all to huddle up closely, so *Team Delta Force* could not hear our game plan.

Jaden began to talk in a whisper to us saying, "O.K. this is how we are going to beat them…"

Before we knew it, the time was 1:00, and Dr. B. strolled down the third baseline. He came to home plate and signaled for all of us to gather round.

"Alright, who will be our two team leaders for this event today?" he asked.

"I'm going to lead *Team Delta Force* to our first victory," Adam said arrogantly.

"What makes you think you are assured to win this event Adam?" Dr. B. asked.

"Not only am I the captain of the school soccer team, I probably have the strongest legs of anyone on both teams. *Team L.O.T.* will never get me out, let alone the rest of the athletes on *Team Delta Force*," Adam said with a swagger to his voice.

"We'll see Adam if your prediction is overconfidence or reality at the end of the day. Let's hear from Team L.O.T. Who will your captain be?" Dr. B. asked.

Jaden stood straight up, and proudly said, "I am going to be the team leader for our team today sir."

"You say that with much vigor and pride," Dr. B. said.

"I believe the other members who led us inspired me to stand up and lead the team when the time was right. I believe that time for me is now," Jaden replied.

Adam and Alex started chuckling at Jaden's reply, and both shouted out in tandem, "Brown nose!"

Dr. B. turned to Alex and Adam and was about to say something, but it looked like he regained his composure, and stated, "It takes a lot of courage to stand up in front of a crowd and volunteer to lead. When members of a team start taking the lead, it is one tell tale sign that your team is being led in the right direction. Then, there are teams who are sitting in a three foot hole, and do not know how to see their way out of the hole. They complain or mock others, when all they have to do to find their way out is for someone to just stand up!"

Dr. B. then turned to everyone and yelled, "Let's play ball!"

Jaden didn't look as fit as Adam, but I knew appearances can be deceiving. When Jaden walked, he either had a limp or he strutted like he was confident. He always wore baggy sweats and a baggy sweatshirt to camp each day. He was very self-conscious when any of us wanted to help him stretch out for each competitive event. He always gently replied that he didn't need any help stretching out. Jaden always seemed to really study and focus on how to approach each event every time we practiced in the morning. I thought he was a good pick to lead us in this event. Plus, I liked how he placed each of us on the field and in the batting line up.

Jaden talked to everyone before he placed him or her at each position and before he created the batting order. He wanted to make sure he knew everybody's strengths and weaknesses. He wanted to make sure he had the right people in the right places, which is the "*Assemble*" step we learned yesterday.

We all could taste victory because we not only had a leader whom we believed in, but he made sure he applied everything he had learned the three previous days. Jaden said he would play catcher because he could view the whole field from the other team's perspective when they were at the plate. We were ready to play. Dr. B. said since we had won the last two days, we get to be the home team. We took the field first and *Team Delta Force* was up at the plate.

Chris rolled the first pitch to Adam. When he kicked the ball, the tone was set for the majority of the game. "THUD!" That was the sound of my heart falling into my stomach when I saw Adam kick the ball so far into left field that he could have walked around the bases. I thought Adam's homerun was just pure luck; however, that all changed when at the end of the first inning, the score was *Team Delta Force*—Four and *Team L.O.T.*—Zero.

The homerun streak continued for *Team Delta Force.* At the end of the fourth inning, the score was now ten to nothing in favor of *Team Delta Force*. I thought to myself that Jaden better do some leading real soon or this game is going to get out of hand!

"Everyone huddle up at the bench," Jaden replied with a very frustrated tone. "We need to make some changes fast because we only have two innings left. We need to score eleven runs to win, and still hold them from scoring the last two innings. Any observations out in the field or while we're batting?" Jaden asked.

"They only score runs when a few of their guys are up. They keep kicking the ball over our heads in the outfield all the time," Jacob said.

"Anyone else have any input," Jaden asked.

"I have one observation. When we're up to kick, we always pop out. We never get on base," Isabella said in a gentle and honest tone of voice.

"O.K. great input, Jacob and Isabella. Let's take what both of them said, and combine it with some things I observed so far. We can still win this, but we all have to work together. We need to execute our new strategy when the time is right whether we are in the field or are kicking," Jaden said.

He continued, by whispering, "Listen up! This is what we will do to win…"

Before they knew it, the score was now ten to seven and the bases were loaded with two outs in the bottom of the last inning. Jaden was up next to kick. Adam and Alex were teasing Jaden by calling him "Lefty" because Jaden would always kick the ball down the left field line with his right foot every time he was up.

"Come on Lefty. Gee, I wonder where 'Lefty' is going to kick the ball this time?" Adam shouted with a smirk on his face.

As predicted, Jaden kicked the first two balls down the third base line, but both were foul balls.

Alex jumped into the mix and shouted, "Hey 'Lefty.' I think your leading days are over. You'll never even make it to first base. We're going to name this next defensive move after you."

All of a sudden, Alex waived their right fielder over to play behind the third basemen and the short stop to prevent any balls from getting through. This left right field wide open for the picking.

Angelina from *Team Delta Force* rolled the ball to Jaden, but the strangest thing happened. Instead of kicking the ball with is right foot, Jaden kicked it with his left foot. And, instead of kicking it down the third baseline like every other kick during the game, he kicked the ball into right field. Not just into right field! Jaden kicked the ball so far into right field, he walked around the bases and literally won the game with a walk off grand slam. Everyone's jaw on *Team Delta Force* literally hit the ground when they saw Jaden walk across home plate, and had realized they just lost their third consecutive event.

"Kudos, Jaden! Kudos," exclaimed Dr. B.

"Now that is a perfect example of not only 'Talking the Talk', but literally 'Walking the Walk'!" said Dr. B.

He continued, by saying, "I must say I had doubts when the score was ten to nothing, but I noticed you all regrouped at the top of the fifth inning. What gives?"

Jaden began to speak, by saying, "I implemented what you had taught us the first three days, but I realized it was not enough to lead my team to victory. Just because you have the right people in the right places is not enough to win. They also have to know when to do the right things at the right time. I had made some observations, but I needed to hear from other people what they thought was occurring. Their responses confirmed my suspicions, so we created a new strategy."

Jaden continued, by saying, "The strategy was to play deep on defense because all the guys were trying to kick homeruns on *Team Delta Force*. That was their only way of scoring on us. We played deep and they popped out. On offense, we popped out all the time because we tried to follow *Team Delta Force's* strategy, but we tried too hard, and made a lot of dumb kicks. We all decided just to focus on getting on base, and kick with our minds and not our hearts. Next thing you know it, we were stringing base hits together and scoring points. As for my last at bat, it was a strategy I was concocting all along, and would only use it when the time was right. Which gets back to what you hinted to us yesterday about doing the *right things at the right time*."

"What right thing was that?" Dr. B. asked with baited breath.

Jaden hesitated to respond at first and then he responded by saying, "You see. I did purposely kick the ball to left field all the time as a strategy, but I didn't sandbag any of those kicks. I couldn't kick the ball as far as my left leg could because of my prosthetic right leg!" At that moment, Jaden pulled up his right sweat pant leg and revealed his prosthetic leg. At first, I was shocked, but that all faded as he went on to finish his story.

Jaden continued, by saying, "I had a feeling that *Team Delta Force* would do something corny like they did to me by shifting people around to defend my kicks. The *time was right* with the bases loaded, so I decided to kick the ball with my left leg to the wide open right field."

But, then Jaden said the funniest thing. "Oh by the way Adam and Alex, my left leg is stronger than most human beings legs because I have to compensate for only having one leg, so I don't mind being called 'Lefty.' That's why I was able to kick the ball not only deep into right field, but also farther than any of your kicks went." Dr. B. started to chuckle, but he quickly regained his composure to point out how Jaden had stumbled upon step four of becoming a good leader.

Dr. B. began talking, by saying, "Jaden stumbled upon step four, which I call '*Discuss*." What I mean by this is that a good leader always *discusses or shares his vision*. He does not lecture. A leader tries to lift his people's vision to a higher sight and a higher standard of performance. A leader accomplishes this by always involving his members and receiving input, so that the end result is a shared vision and not just the vision of the leader.

Jaden took the time to reevaluate his vision or strategy in the beginning. Unknowingly, Jaden realized his original strategy or vision was not working because no one knew the game plan. They thought having the right players in the right position was enough to win."

Dr. B. continued, by saying, "Jaden asked for everyone's input at the beginning of the fifth inning because a new strategy was needed to win. By asking for everyone's input, he was basically asking everyone to share in the new vision. Everyone did buy into the new strategy or vision because it was a shared vision that was *discussed* among all members. The last play of the game was just sheer genius. I guess one might say that Jaden not only can do the right thing at the right time, but also the 'Left' thing at the right time!"

Everyone on *Team L.O.T.* was laughing at Dr. B.'s play on words, but there was bitter silence emanating from *Team Delta Force*.

"So, now you know the first four steps of being a good leader. They are *Look, Envision, Assemble,* and *Discuss*. Tomorrow we will learn the fifth step before our first week comes to an end. Here is a hint as to what you will be doing and learning tomorrow. When playing for a team, one cannot capture the title and wave the flag in victory if you do not know when to step onto the field and when to step off the field," Dr. B. said.

He finished, by saying, "Think about this. I will see all of you tomorrow on the football field at 9 A.M. sharp." Dr. B. then turned and walked off the baseball field and disappeared behind the bleachers. We were puzzled about his hints, but we all couldn't wait for tomorrow to come soon enough.

Chapter Summary

- Step 4 in becoming a leader is the ability to *"Discuss the Vision."*
- A good leader always *discusses or shares his vision*. He does not lecture. A leader tries to lift his people's vision to a higher sight and a higher standard of performance. A leader accomplishes this by always involving his members and receiving input so that the end result is a shared vision and not just the vision of the leader.
- Putting the right people in the right places is no good unless they know how to do the right thing at the right time.
- When members of a team start taking the lead, it is one tell tale sign that your team is being led in the right direction.

Chapter 6
Empower the Team

"Empowerment saturates. Absolute empowerment saturates absolutely." (Dave Tantillo)

It was Friday, and the last day of the first week of Leadership Camp. I can't believe I made it through without complaining once. Our team of misfits has out played, and out maneuvered a team loaded with athletes jammed packed with beauty, brawn, and athleticism. I wonder what today's lesson is, and what competitive event we'll have to perform before the week ends. Looks like we'll know in a minute because here comes Dr. B. walking onto the field. And, you probably can guess what he is wearing. Yep! Dr. B. is wearing his patented velour gym suit, which is sporting a rosy shade of red.

"Good morning young men and women! Today we will be learning the fifth step of becoming a good leader. To learn this step, you will be competing against each other in a game called 'Capture the Flag.' If you do not know how to play, then here you go.

Each team will own one half of the football field. Each team will tie their flag to their respective goal post. The object is to capture the opposing team's flag and bring it back to your half of the field without being touched while you are on the opposing team's half of the field. If you get touched while in the opposing side of the field, with or without the flag in hand, you will be immediately sent to the opposing team's prison. You can be freed if one of your players runs to the prison and touches you without being touched by the opposing team.

The game is all about strategy and speed. You better have your running shoes on and your thinking caps on at the same time, or you will end up in prison or flagless in the end. You know the usual routine for this morning. Practice, and I will see you all at 1:00," Dr. B. said. He turned around, walked off the field, and headed back to the high school.

We immediately went to work to find out who would like to be the next team leader for today's event. After a ten-minute discussion, our team came to the unanimous decision that Emily would be our next team leader. Emily was very small in stature. She stood at best five feet tall on a good day and was quite thin. She had short bobbed, curly, black hair and had a bubbly personality. She appeared to be the preppy girl type because her wardrobe seemed to be solely constructed of plaid. She loved gymnastics, but had to quit after five years because her parents couldn't afford to send her anymore.

Her parents sent her to Leadership Camp because they felt guilty not letting her continue with gymnastics. They wanted her to do something this summer, and found out they could afford this camp. She said she was mad at first, but after all we have done this week she is glad they sent her.

The time flew so fast today that I looked at the clock on the football scoreboard and it said 12:58. I turned to the high school and bursting through the doors came Dr. B. He made his way onto the field and as predicted he started out the conversation with his usual request.

"Alright, who will be our two team leaders for this event today?" Dr. B. asked inquisitively.

"I will be *Team Delta Force*'s team leader today Dr. B." said Destiny in her flirtatious voice.

"And why you Destiny?" Dr. B. asked.

"I guess that I am the best female on the team at capturing the hearts of young men, so who better to lead at capturing a measly, simple, little flag tied around a pole? Young men are much tougher to capture!" Destiny replied with a smirk on her face. Dr. B. had no rebuttal for Destiny's response. He just turned to us and asked who our team leader was going to be today.

"I will be *Team L.O.T.*'s leader today." Emily said with a confident smile.

"And, why are you going to be the team leader today?" Dr. B. asked.

"For two reasons, Dr. B. First, I have really enjoyed the first four days, and I too felt it was time for me to step up and be the team leader. And secondly, I'm a flag girl in the school's marching band. So, who better than a flag girl should know all about flags," Emily responded in her bubbly voice.

Dr. B. chuckled, and responded with, "I'm not sure being a flag girl qualifies you for being a team leader in this event, but I'll reserve my judgment in the end. I've learned not to question your team's logic because you seem to be making all the right choices so far." Of course Alex from the other team had to make a sarcastic remark about Emily.

"I think the only thing Emily is qualified for is to be a munchkin in the Wizard of Oz." Alex said as he laughed with his other teammates. Destiny could not pass up the opportunity to add to Alex's wisecracks.

"The only thing you'll capture today is a glimpse of our team buzzing by you with your flag because you'll be watching the whole scene from our prison," Destiny blurted sarcastically.

Emily paused for a moment and replied to Destiny and Alex by saying, "It's not the size of the dog in the fight that wins. It's the size of the fight in the dog that wins every time!"

Dr. B. added a warning, by stating, "Don't judge a book by its cover. Emily might be small in size, but I bet her determination to win is quite large."

Dr. B. backed off the field, and shouted, "Let the game begin!"

The first part of Emily's strategy was to play defense, and not to go onto *Team Delta Force's* side of the field initially. She wanted to pick off most of their team members before attacking. Plus, she believed it would take all of us to even catch a few of them on our side because *Team Delta Force* was loaded with athletes.

It didn't take long before *Team Delta Force* figured out what we were trying to do. It appeared to be a stalemate for a moment where neither team would enter the opposing field. Chris ran up to Emily, and wanted to ask her something.

"Emily, I have an idea! Do you mind if I can make a suggestion to add to your strategy?" Chris said quietly and anxiously. Emily was open to any suggestions.

"Go for it Chris!" said Emily.

"I've been studying everyone on *Team Delta Force.* I truly think they would not be able to catch me if it were just a few of them chasing me. I know I can outrun them. Trust me. What do you think?" Chris asked excitedly.

Emily paused for a moment, and said, "O.K., I trust you, but you'll need a diversion so only a few will chase after you." Emily ran to each *Team L.O.T.* member, and told tell them the plan.

When she had finished telling the last member, she yelled out, "O.D.!" This stood for Operation Diversion.

Immediately Emily dropped back to guard the prison, and everyone else but Chris rushed down the left side of the field. Chris was left one on one with Logan on the right side of the field. Like a bullet, Chris bolted pass Logan, and now was headed for the goal post. Destiny was guarding their prison, and noticed Chris getting real close to the flag tied on their goal post. She immediately screamed to Alex and the other members of *Team Delta Force* to come quickly. I couldn't believe that Chris's suggestion was going to work like a charm. *Team Delta Force* fell into our trap, and soon would be going down in defeat again.

Then, it happened! We should have seen it coming, but we kept forgetting that *Team Delta Force* loves to stretch the rules. Chris's plan not only failed miserably, but it sent the fastest person on our team straight to jail.

Chris had the biggest smile on his face when he was approaching the goal post, but as he got closer his face turned to confusion and then terror. Apparently, *Team Delta Force* didn't just tie their flag to the goal post. They tied their flag ten feet high on the goal post where not one of us could ever get to it. By the time Chris realized he couldn't capture the flag, all the members of *Team Delta Force* surrounded him. He was tagged right away and sent to prison.

Chris was screaming to us that they tied it up ten feet high while he was walking to prison. Everyone on *Team Delta Force* was hysterically laughing about how everything went down. They could see the shock, fear, and discouragement on our faces now. We not only lost our fastest player, but we had no clue how to get the flag that was ten feet high.

Emily did the next best thing a good leader should do. Have the team regroup and tell everyone we're still sticking to the original strategy of being conservative by playing from a defensive position. No one is to go onto the opposing field until the time is right. We are only one man down. There are still nine of us and we'll figure out a way to get that flag.

But, that all changed when Ben asked Emily to plan an attack, so he can maneuver his way to the goal post. He believed with his height and jumping ability that he would get the flag. She agreed to his suggestion, but when the dust settled Ben, Olivia, and Isabella were captured, and put in prison. Ben's plan failed also. We were now down to only six players left on *Team L.O.T.*

It didn't look good for us. *Team Delta Force* was mocking us, and baiting us to try some other brainy idea to get their flag. Then, in the corner of my eye, I saw Jill whisper something to Emily, while she was guarding the prison. Emily listened and immediately ran up to midfield just slightly remaining on our side so she would not get tagged. She started mouthing off to Alex. She was saying things to Alex that would normally come from his mouth.

Everyone on both sides ran up to midfield to join in the ruckus, except for Jill. I didn't want to turn around to give the other team a heads-up as to what we were doing, but she was up to something. Jill eventually made her way back up to midfield to join the rest of us within a minute or so.

Emily had Alex fuming so bad with what she was saying to him that before he could start going off on her she immediately walked away and waved everyone to regroup.

Emily began to speak with authority and assuredness, by saying, "It's now or never, everyone. Listen up! Everyone but Jill and I spread out and make a full assault on getting that flag. When I say go, take off like a bat out of hell!"

Jacob immediately interrupted Emily, by saying, "That's mass suicide! We are outnumbered, and a lot slower than them. Plus, we haven't figured out how to get the flag yet! Please tell me there is a part two to this strategy."

"There is a part two. We don't have time to explain. They're all ticked off right now, so they're not in the right frame of mind. Jill came up with a full proof plan. Listen closely! You have to prove to them that you are really trying to get to the flag. I'll trust all four of you that you'll give your best performance yet, and we hope you'll trust Jill and I that we'll give our best performance yet. Any questions?" Emily asked.

There was a moment of silence at first. Then, Jacob, Grace, Jaden and I started to spread out and scream like a bunch of maniacs. Next, all four of us looked at each other, and with a nod of the head took off with our eyes focused on getting that flag.

Within thirty seconds all four of us were captured and put into prison. I was now watching the game from *Team Delta Force's* prison, and it didn't look pretty. It was Jill and Emily against all of *Team Delta Force*. Then, something weird happened. Jill and Emily called Alex, Destiny and the rest of *Team Delta Force* up to midfield.

There was an exchange of words, and then both groups ran by without tagging each other heading towards each other's flags. I was totally confused like the rest of us were in prison. Even if Jill and Emily got to the flag neither one of them could jump ten feet in the air and remove the flag. Why are they even wasting their time?

I decided to turn my eyes toward our flag, and *Team Delta Force's* decent upon it. Then, the most bizarre and hilarious thing happened all at once. Alex was leading the charge and it appeared he would be the first one to capture our flag. In a full sprint, he reached out for our flag. He grabbed the flag as though he would rip it off and run down the field screaming victory, but this is where the most bizarre and hilarious thing occurred.

Apparently, when he grabbed the flag, it remained on the pole and yanked Alex back from his full sprint causing him to land flat on his back empty handed! The other team members were not concerned about Alex being hurt because they were all trying to remove the flag furiously. Somehow, they kept failing at every attempt to untie the flag from our pole. Meanwhile, Alex was still lying on the ground trying to regain his senses after his fall. Something didn't seem right. Why couldn't they remove the flag?

Before I could figure out the answer, I saw in the corner of my eye Jill and Emily walking back to midfield with the flag in their hand. What is going on? Before I knew it, Dr. B. was blowing his whistle and yelling that the game is over and that *Team L.O.T.* has won. Dr. B. waved both teams to come to the center of midfield.

"I cannot believe what I just saw. You two pulled off the most amazing victory and stunt I've ever seen in capture the flag. You have to tell the rest of us how you concocted such a plan, let alone how you were able to pull it off?" Dr. B. asked in amazement.

Destiny immediately screamed, "You guys cheated! You tied the flag some way with some stupid knot so we couldn't take it off."

"Stop the press!" said Dr. B. with a serious tone.

He continued, by stating, "*Team L.O.T.* acted within the rules. Just like you did when you decided to tie your flag ten feet high, knowing one person alone could not untie the flag. Remember those who live in glass houses should not throw stones. I guess Emily captured more than just a glimpse of *Team Delta Force.* She captured your pride as well as your flag!" Destiny immediately shut up, but I could tell she was fuming with anger.

"Emily could you please share with us how you did it?" Dr. B. asked curiously.

"My strategy from the beginning was to play conservatively and defensively until we could come up with a plan to some how capture their flag. Chris asked me if we could try his plan of creating a diversion, so he could outrun his opponent and capture their flag. I wasn't sure if it was going to work, but I trusted him and we did as he asked, but failed in the attempt. I believe his plan would've worked if *Team Delta Force* did not tie their flag ten feet high.

Our next plan came from Ben. He suggested to me to create a full frontal assault. He believed between his height and his jumping ability he would be able to capture the flag. Once again, I wasn't sure if it was going to work, but I trusted him. We not only failed to get the flag, but we lost three more people in the attack. I was running out of options and then a little bird whispered in my ear." Emily said in a laughing way.

"What do you mean a little bird whispered in your ear?" Dr. B. asked.

Emily continued, by saying, "The little bird was Jill. She had an idea. She asked me if I trusted her. And, I told her at that very moment I would be open to any suggestions because our winning streak was about to come to an abrupt end. Jill asked me to charge to midfield and start getting Alex all riled up.

This would serve two purposes. First, it created a distraction for Jill to tie our flag again on the pole. Second, it would get Alex and the rest of *Team Delta Force* in an aggressive state of mind, so they could not see the trap we were about to set."

"What trap was that?" asked Destiny in a bitter tone.

Emily continued, by saying, "The trap was to get you guys riled up first. Then, tell the remaining members on our team except Jill and I to attack all at once. Knowing my team members would all get caught, we hoped *Team Delta Force* would believe they were in a win-win position seeing there were only Jill and I remaining.

The last part of the trap was luring *Team Delta Force* into making a bad decision. We challenged them by saying Jill and I could capture their flag quicker than all ten of them capturing our flag. Banking on the fact they were all riled up now and the fact their egos were larger than life, *Team Delta Force* accepted our challenge without batting an eyelash. The rest was history!"

"Wait a minute," said Dr. B.

He continued, by saying, "You didn't explain to everyone what caused *Team Delta Force* to fail, and how you and Jill captured the flag that was tied ten feet high when you both standing on each others shoulders barely stand nine feet tall." Emily looked at Jill and started to laugh.

With a smile on her face, Emily said, "That was nothing. The plan was schemed up totally by Jill again. The plan had two parts. First, Jill needed to do something to buy us some time so we could attempt to execute part two, which was capture *Team Delta Force's* flag. Jill tied the flag again, but this time using a sailor's knot. (It just so happens, Jill's father loves to sail. Her father happened to teach Jill how to perform a sailor's knot.) There is only one way to untie the knot. She was banking on the fact no one on *Team Delta Force* would know how to untie it.

It was apparent and funny at the same time. Apparent because their whole team was huddled around the pole fighting over how to remove the flag, and no one could do it. It was funny because Alex fell flat on his butt thinking he would be the chosen one to remove the flag like Sir Lancelot removing the sword from the stone."

Everyone on *Team L.O.T.* chuckled and even some on *Team Delta Force* chuckled at Emily's last comment. Emily continued after everyone stopped laughing.

"The icing on the cake was part two of the plan. How do two short girls untie a flag ten feet high? Simple. Jill got to the pole first and leaned her back hard against it facing towards me. She stretched both of her arms down and cupped both her hands together to form a kind of stirrup. She yelled to me to run full force at her like I was doing a gymnastic routine. In full stride, I placed one foot in her stirrup and leaped as high as I could, while she lifted with all her might.

And, wouldn't you know it, it worked like a charm. I leaped so high that the flag was at my waist. No one saw us because everyone believed *Team Delta Force* would get our flag first. Everyone believed we had no chance to get their flag, so eyes were on them. I couldn't have done it without Jill. I trusted her. I guess sometimes as a leader you have to know when to let others lead if you want to win the game," said Emily.

"Bingo! That's it!" said Dr. B. with a smile on his face.

"What's what?" asked Emily.

"Step five of how to become a good leader...*Empowerment*!" said Dr. B.

"What's empowerment, Dr. B.?" asked Emily.

Dr. B. responded, by saying, "The best leaders are always those who know they haven't got all the answers to a situation. They also realize that (*Assembling a team*) putting the right people in the right places and (*Discussing the vision*) teaching them do the right things at the right time is still not enough. They need to know when to step back and trust that the right people will deliver the vision. This is where *Empowerment* comes in to play."

"I think I know what you mean, but can you give me an example of *Empowerment*?" asked Emily.

Dr. B. replied, by saying, "Sure. Let's look at the football example I used when I taught you guys about step three—*Assembling the team*. A good coach, who is also a good leader, does three things to get his team ready. First, he *Assembles* the right players in the right positions. Second, he *Discusses* the game plan with them, so they know when to do the right things at the right time.

Finally, he knows when to walk off the field, and let the players play the game. Thus, he basically *Empowers* them to execute the game plan. The players now have the freedom to take charge and make decisions. It is crystal clear to them what the rules are, what is their territory, and what the playing field looks like."

"Now, I get it. I empowered Chris, Ben, and Jill to execute their plans. I stepped back, so they could help our team win." Emily said with a smile on her face.

"Exactly Emily, but once again *Empowerment* is still not enough to become a good leader. Here's a hint for next Monday's lesson and competitive event. What happens when a leader lets his *Empowered* soldiers keep losing every battle they engage in? The end result is just a group of highly trained infantry who are just dodging bullets and never advancing on a beachhead. Have a great weekend. I will see everyone in the gym at 9AM sharp!" Dr. B. said.

He turned around and marched off the field like a field general leaving his battalion to think about his words of wisdom. I guess we'll see what General Patton has in store for us next week!

Chapter Summary

- Step 5 in becoming a leader is the ability to "*Empower the Team.*"
- A good leader is one who knows she doesn't have all the answers to a situation. Putting the right people in the right places and teaching them to do the right things at the right time is still not enough. A good leader knows when to step back and trust that the right people will deliver the vision.

- A good leader performs three things to get her team ready:
  - 1.) *Assemble* the right players in the right positions.
  - 2.) *Discuss* the game plan with them, so they know when to do the right things at the right time.
  - 3.) *Empower* the players by walking off the field, so the players can execute the game plan.
- A good leader allows her players to have the freedom to take charge and make decisions. It is crystal clear to the players what the rules are, what is their territory, and what the playing field looks like.
- It's not the size of the dog in the fight that wins. It's the size of the fight in the dog that wins every time!

Chapter 7
Reinforce the Positive

"Hearing positive comments can reinforce your worth and can promote a stronger willingness to work for success." (Carl Mays—author of *Anatomy of a Leader*)

Monday could not come soon enough for me or the other members on my team. We were all talking about how much fun we had last week, especially at the expense of *Team Delta Force*. We really looked forward to finishing the week and learning all ten steps that would help us become good leaders. None of us could decipher the hint Dr.B. gave us on Friday about what we would be learning today or even what activity we would be performing. We would know soon though because he suddenly burst through the gym doors.

Stop the presses! Dr. B. just walked into the gym, but there was something different this time. No more colorful, velour gym outfits. Dr. B. was actually wearing a cool looking black Nike® gym outfit. No one said anything at first, but that soon changed when Alex from *Team Delta Force* had to make a wise crack.

"What gives, Dr. B?" Alex asked sarcastically.

"What do you mean, Alex?" asked Dr.B.

"How come you're not sporting your 1970's colorful velour gym suit look today?" Alex asked again with a smirk on his face.

"Was something wrong with what I was wearing last week?" Dr. B. asked Alex.

"Yeah! Didn't you ever hear about dressing for success? I would think that if you're going to teach about being a leader, one should dress like a leader," Alex replied.

"I thought he looked cute last week. Plus, who cares what he wears. Clothes don't make a man. The man inside the clothes makes a man. It's kind of like what Dr. Martin Luther King said. Don't judge me by the color of the clothes I wear, but by the content of my character," Olivia said with conviction.

Dr. B. responded, by saying, "Not exactly what Dr. King said, but I understand what you meant. Alex…here is some free advice on being a leader. Once again, don't judge a book by its cover! Pope John Paul II wore his clerical garb. General MacArthur wore his military attire. Jack Welch (former CEO of General Electric) wore a suit. Nelson Mandella wore prison clothes. Jesus wore a simple robe. There is no set apparel that qualifies you as a leader. All were or still are great leaders, but each one wore different styles of clothes. Some clothes are worn by the wealthy. Some clothes are worn by the poor. Are you getting the picture Alex?"

"Yes, I get it. Is that why you changed clothes this week? Did you want to see if we noticed your wardrobe change and hopefully make some kind of off-color remark?" asked Alex.

"Exactly, Alex! However, there is something else I wanted to teach you with regards to the clothes I wore last week. It isn't what you wear that helps you become a leader, it is what you say and do that helps you become a leader." Dr. B. said.

"Speaking of saying and doing, thank you for the kind words and sticking up for my attire Olivia. This is a perfect segue to today's topic. What do you do as a leader when the right people are in the right place doing the right thing at the right time, but their results are not exactly how you want them to be? What should a good leader say and do?" Dr. B. asked.

He continued, by saying, "I don't want an answer now, but think about it as you play your competitive event today."

"What are we going to play today?" asked Logan from *Team Delta Force*.

"Get your knee pads and elbow pads on because you're going to play some Dodge Ball." Dr. B. said. As usual, you will have all morning to practice. I will return at 1:00 to ask for each team leader, and then we'll engage in today's competitive event.

Team L.O.T. migrated over to one side of the gym and *Team Delta Force* just naturally migrated over to the opposing side. We started right away with figuring out who would lead us next. There were five of us who had not been a team leader yet: Chris, Jacob, Isabella, Olivia and I. I was about to step up when all of a sudden Olivia popped the question.

"If everyone doesn't mind, I would like to be the team leader for this event. Is that OK with everyone?" Olivia asked. How could I say "No" when she asked so nicely? Plus, I didn't have the courage to speak up as she did!

"I second the motion," said Jill.

"All in favor?" asked Chris.

We all voted in unison by saying "Yes" to Chris's motion. Looks like I'll have to wait another day before I can take the plunge and become our team leader.

Olivia was a Native American girl who was quiet and very even keeled. She stood close to six feet tall and had an awkward body frame. She was not heavy by any standard, but she was big-boned. When she walked, she seemed to be very carefree, and very slow in her stride. She was not a person who seemed to be in a hurry. She had a homely face and haircut, but her smile and personality generated so much warmth that you never even noticed her awkward physical features. I wondered why she wanted to lead us in this event. Immediately Olivia jumped into her team leader role by teaching us how to catch and throw balls.

"Hey. How do you know how to catch and throw a ball? Have you ever played Dodge Ball before?" asked Jacob.

"Yes, but only for fun in school gym class." Olivia said with her warm smile.

She continued, by saying, "Listen up everybody. This is going to be a painful and challenging event for us to win. We need to stick together even if the odds are against us. They have oodles of athletic ability, but Dodge Ball is not always about athletic ability. This is what we will do this afternoon…"

* * *

When 1:00 rolled around, I think my team was a little uneasy as to how well we would do. We understood that as fun as Dodge Ball sounded, it was going to be painful whether we won or lost. Getting hit by a dodge ball was quite a stinging experience, especially if you get hit up close and on an exposed area of your body. Dr. B. walked into the room dragging a huge netted bag of red dodge balls.

"Here you go everyone," Dr. B. said as he was emptying the balls from his bag.

He continued, by saying, "Who are our team leaders today and why? Let's hear from *Team L.O.T.* first this time."

"I'll be the team leader for this event for our team" said Olivia calmly and proudly.

"May I ask if you volunteered or were selected by your team?" asked Dr. B.

"I volunteered because I felt that I could lead the team in this event," said Olivia.

"Why is that?" asked Dr. B.

"I've played some recreational Dodge Ball before. I understand the basics, and I thought I could help my team. Plus, it was my turn to take a stand, and lead my team like everyone else has been doing," Olivia said proudly in her melancholy voice.

"The only standing you'll be doing is standing on the sidelines while you watch your team members get picked off one-by-one by us," Brooke said arrogantly.

"Let me guess, Brooke. You're going to be *Team Delta Force's* next team leader?" Dr. B. asked, but already knew what the response was going to be.

"Yep! I'm going to be the team leader. I can throw a dodge ball quite fast because I pitch for the high school fast pitch softball team. By the way, Olivia loves dodge ball because they named it after her," Brooke said in a mean voice.

"What's that supposed to mean?" Jill replied in an angry voice.

"Well, she is built like a Dodge® truck. Look at the size of her!" Brooke replied and started laughing with the rest of *Team Delta Force.*

"That's ENOUGH!" Dr. B. yelled, as he started to walk between both teams. He sensed there was a ruckus that was about to unfold.

"Haven't you guys learned your lesson yet about calling names or acting childish? If you think it's a ploy to intimidate your competition, it hasn't worked yet. So, drop the attitude from this point on, or my attitude will drop on you!" Dr. B. said sternly as he looked at *Team Delta Force*.

He continued, by saying, "Everyone go to his or her respective sides. When I blow my whistle, let the competition begin."

Dr. B. raised his right hand slowly in the air. He then grabbed his whistle with his left hand. With calculated hesitation, he looked at both teams and with a deep-breathe he blew the whistle so hard that it looked like he wanted to scream at that moment. The game was now on!

Immediately *Team Delta Force* came out and grabbed more balls than we did. The next moment a barrage of red balls came our way fast and furious. After the first wave of throws from *Team Delta Force*, we reciprocated but as suspected our feeble attempts at trying to pick them off all at once did not go as planned. After the first ten minutes, the number of *Team L.O.T.* members on the floor was dwindling fast.

"What should we do, Olivia? We're outnumbered now. The only guy left on our side is Chris because he is the fastest and can dodge the balls quickly," Isabella said with great concern.

"O.K., listen up, everyone. Follow behind me. I'm going to shield you guys, so you can attack when the timing is right. I will deflect all the throws with this ball in my hand. When we get to mid-court, jump out from behind me and throw as hard as you can," Olivia said out of the side of her mouth, so *Team Delta Force* could not hear her.

Like a bull in a china shop, Olivia charged forward deflecting all of *Team Delta Force's* throws. It was unbelievable. It was like she was parting the Red Sea because there were so many balls being thrown at her that all I saw was the color red. As soon as Olivia got to mid-court, Isabella, Chris, and Jill jumped out and threw their balls with all their might. Unfortunately, Olivia's plan backfired.

Isabella's throw was so weak that Angelina caught her throw, which eliminated her first. When Chris jumped out, *Team Delta Force* was ready and set a trap for him. Chris focused so much on throwing at Alex to get him out that he was blindsided. Logan snuck up from the other side of the court and zeroed in on Chris the whole time. He struck Chris on the back while Chris was trying to hit Alex and eliminate him from the game.

It was down to Jill and Olivia to win it for *Team L.O.T.*, but our situation went from bad to worse in an ugly way. When Jill jumped out, she saw Isabella and Chris get eliminated right away. She hesitated in throwing her ball, so she and Olivia could regroup and come up with another strategy. Then it happened!

Jill noticed that Alex was about to throw his ball at Olivia point blank on her blind side. Olivia was too distracted to notice Alex creeping up because she was trying to deflect all the throws coming at her. Jill had to act quickly to prevent Olivia from being knocked out. So, she did the only thing she could do to help her team. As Alex cocked his hand back and started to throw his ball at Olivia, Jill did the most courageous thing I ever saw during camp. She jumped in front of Olivia to protect her and got struck in the head by Alex's ball!

THUD! That was the sound of Jill's body hitting the floor because the ball knocked Jill off balance. Dr. B. immediately blew his whistle and called a time out. I came running over first to see if Jill was hurt. Dr. B. was close behind. Jill was a little groggy from the hit, but appeared to be OK. As Dr. B. and I were helping Jill off the court, Olivia asked Jill why she jumped in harms way for her.

Jill replied in her soft, but groggy voice, "You're our leader. We need you in the game for us to win."

Olivia said, "I'm the only one left. It's ten against one. What can I do?"

Jill stopped walking off the court, looked Olivia straight in her eyes, and said, "We may not be on the floor with you right now, but it doesn't mean you're all alone in the game. You'll find a way for us to win. I believe in you!"

The most bizarre thing happened next. Olivia's face went through a series of facial expressions as she was walking to the back of the court on our side. When she turned around to face everyone again to start the game, the look on her face this time was not the same calm, cool, and collected Olivia we knew. She looked angry and determined to prove something.

Everyone on *Team Delta Force* was laughing about what happened to Jill. They were making some snide remarks about how this was going to be an easy win now. They were all yelling at Olivia in hope the intimidating comments would cause her to mess up and get hit. Our whole team started screaming and cheering for Olivia to do her best. We kept yelling we believed in her.

Then, as though a veil of peacefulness fell upon Olivia, her normal calm-looking face returned. She looked directly at us, winked, and she placed the ball that was in her hands down to the ground. She was now empty handed and at the mercy of *Team Delta Force.* At least we thought that until the impossible happened.

As soon as Olivia placed the ball down on the ground, Destiny threw her ball and Olivia caught it. Immediately Jaden jumped back into the game. One-by-one, Olivia was a catching machine. She was catching all the throws from the members of *Team Delta Force.* She had caught so many balls that almost our whole team was now back on the floor and the only remaining members from *Team Delta Force* were Alex and Brooke.

They both were scrambling now because they didn't know what to do. They were now outnumbered nine to two. Then, out of nowhere came a throw from behind me that flew past me like a rocket ship. The ball hit Brooke so hard in the legs that it knocked her off balance and sent her flying into Alex. Alex naturally caught her from falling. But in his haste to catch her, he sealed his fate. With both of his hands holding onto Brooke, Alex got bombarded like a prisoner standing in front of a firing squad. All of us on the court drilled Alex from all angles. When the dust settled, *Team L.O.T.* once again stood victorious.

We were all congratulating each other when I asked the team, "Who the heck threw that ball at Brooke?"

Jill said, "That bullet throw came express delivery and courtesy of Olivia!"

"Is that true, Olivia?" I asked.

"Yep! I was holding back my throws until I really needed to rifle one," said Olivia. Dr. B. jumped into the conversation because once again he was blown away by how we won the game.

"I can't figure out if you guys are winning by pure luck or winning by great planning and execution. What gives, Olivia? How did you pull it off when you were the last person on the court for your team?" Dr. B. asked inquisitively.

"Well, Dr. B., it was not great planning that won the game for us. It was the other members on my team that won it for us," Olivia said.

"Please explain, Olivia," Dr. B. asked.

"You see, after my plan failed when I asked the team to run behind me while I deflected balls, I felt that I let the team down with my poor decision. I then hit rock bottom when Jill jumped in front of a throw aimed directly at me. It not only knocked her to the ground, but it could've possibly injured her. At that point, it dawned on me that I may not have what it takes to lead any team," Olivia said with a sad voice.

"What happened next, Olivia?" Dr. B. asked.

"First, it all started with Jill. When she was being carried off the court, she said some positive and kind words to me to put me at ease. But, when she said that she believed in me, I started to think. If she believes in me, then I have to believe in myself if I want to win this game for my team," Olivia said, as she started to raise her voice a little.

"Keep going, Olivia. You're on to something big!" Dr. B. said with excitement.

"The turning point for me was when my whole team was cheering for me from the sidelines. They knew they couldn't be in the game at that moment, but they still rooted me on like I truly had a chance to win. I remembered why I became the team leader in the first place for this event," Olivia said, as though she had an epiphany.

"What was the real reason why you wanted to be the team leader Olivia?" Dr. B. asked very curiously.

"Everyone on my team was stepping up to be the team leader, so I knew my time to lead would come eventually. When you said the event would be Dodge Ball, I knew I could lead my team in this event. Plus, it would probably be a breeze for me," Olivia said confidently.

"And, why would this event be a breeze for you to lead?" Dr. B. asked.

"My father was a professional soccer player. He always used me as his goalie when he practiced. I got hit so many times by his blazing kicks that I had to learn how to catch his kicks rather quickly or suffer from permanent black-n-blue marks all over my body." Olivia said, as though she was still feeling the pain from her father's kicks.

She continued, by saying, "I knew *Team Delta Force* couldn't even throw the ball at one hundredth of the speed of my father's kicks, so catching their throws would be a piece if cake. I knew I could teach people how to catch the balls based on the target practice my father performed on me. The best skill to have in Dodge Ball, if your team cannot throw the ball hard, is to be able to catch any ball thrown at you. I knew I could teach that to all my teammates, and that was the real reason why I chose to lead my team on this event."

"O.K. Now I know how you were able to catch all the balls. How did you learn how to throw the ball lightning quick?" asked Jacob.

Olivia smiled, and then laughed before she answered, by saying, "Oh yeah! I forgot to tell you something else my father taught me. He taught me how to play goalie. As you know goalies need to be able to throw balls fast and at long distances. A soccer ball is much larger than a dodge ball, so throwing a dodge ball was a piece of cake."

"Well, I must say, Olivia, I'm not only impressed by the way you led your team to victory, but I'm impressed that you stumbled upon the sixth step you need to do to become a good leader," Dr. B. said proudly.

"What step was that?" asked Olivia.

"Every good leader needs to know when to *Reinforce* a team member's worth when they are feeling down and discouraged. Please let me explain what I mean by *Reinforcing* a person's worth."

Dr. B. continued, by saying, "There are going to be times when you're leading a team and the vision of the team starts to blur. What I mean by blur is poor results from bad decisions or just getting hit by some unexpected occurrence that you didn't foresee. The normal or human response by anyone is to feel discouraged that you and/or the team have failed or is failing to deliver the original team vision."

"Dr. B., you're probably referring to how I plunged my team into darkness and disarray because of my poor decision to attack *Team Delta Force.* They got hit and eliminated because of me. I also put Jill in harms way. She got injured because of my poor leadership. So, you're correct in that I felt like the lights just went out. I was standing all alone in darkness feeling discouraged and embarrassed," Olivia said with a humble tone.

"You're right on track with explaining what I mean by feeling bad when things go awry while leading a team. But, here is the good news! You and your teammates displayed step six naturally without anyone prompting you. Giving a positive comment when someone does something right is easy. Giving a positive comment when someone does something wrong or when something unanticipated and bad happens is difficult to do," Dr.B. said.

Dr. B. continued with an example, by saying, "Let's use the football example again to illustrate my point of *Reinforcing* teammates with positive comments. Fans always cheer when the home team scores every time. But, fans also cheer two other times that are not so obvious. They cheer when they see the home team moving the football down the field, waiting for the moment or play that could put some points on the scoreboard. They are cheering the progress and not just the final result. However, there is a third reason why fans cheer at the football game."

"What's that, Dr. B.?" Olivia asked.

"Fans cheer when the home team is down, also. It is a fact that when fans cheer for their home team, their cheering generates excitement for the home team players. It is this excitement and enthusiasm, which can propel them to try harder to win the game. Giving positive comments will *Reinforce* one's self-worth. Once you believe in yourself, your willingness and desire to succeed will be a natural by-product," Dr. B. said.

"So, it was Jill's kind words and my teammates cheering from the sideline that *Reinforced* my self-worth and motivated me into believing in myself and believing that I could still have a chance to win. They helped me during my darkest hour as their leader," Olivia said with a grateful tone.

"I look at it this way. Instead of cursing the darkness you were in, you lit a candle with the spark coming from within you," Dr. B. said with a warm smile on his face.

"I guess your right. A peace settled upon me when I was hearing all those positive cheers from my team. It was my turning point as their leader. I started believing again that I could still win the game. I just stepped back and remembered why I wanted to lead the team and why I thought I could win in the first place. I guess *Reinforcing* the positive is the best remedy a leader should have in her pocket when life throws a curve ball. Or, in my case, a dodge ball," Olivia said while chuckling.

"Now *Reinforcing* the positive should always happen, but keep in mind this is not a quick fix for everyone to succeed. It takes time for people to overcome their insecurities. Eventually over time, people will rebuild their self-worth. In Olivia's case, it took her a brief moment, but with others it may take days, months, or even years of hearing positive comments. Just like the old saying about Rome not being built in one day. Self-worth is not built in one day!" Dr. B. said.

"But Dr. B., this is a fast paced world. Isn't a good leader usually judged upon how fast she can get good results? If building self-worth takes a long time sometimes, won't you as a leader fail the majority of the time?" Olivia asked.

"Good question, Olivia! This brings us to your hint for tomorrow's event and next step. Success shouldn't be measured on how fast you get results. Let me poise a question. Why does the tortoise always win the race? The answer to this question will be explored tomorrow afternoon. I will see you all on the track tomorrow," Dr. B. said.

With that, Dr. B. turned away and left the gym. We were again puzzled for a moment trying to decipher his hint, but that subsided quickly as we reveled about our victory today. While I was listening to Olivia thanking us for our kind words and telling us the victory was all due to our cheering, I realized something else about giving positive comments. They *Reinforce* your own self-worth. Plus, positive comments also produce positive results. Now, I wonder what we'll learn tomorrow?

Chapter Summary

- Step 6 in becoming a leader is the ability to "*Reinforce the Positive.*"
- Every good leader knows when to *Reinforce* a team member's worth when they are feeling down and discouraged.
- Giving a positive comment when someone does something right is easy. Giving a positive comment when someone does something wrong is difficult to do.
- Giving positive comments will *Reinforce* one's self-worth. Once you believe in yourself, your willingness and desire to succeed will be a natural by-product.
- *Reinforcing* the positive is the best remedy a leader should have in her pocket when life throws you a curve ball.
- It isn't what you wear that helps you become a leader, it is what you say and do that helps you become a leader.

Chapter 8
Short-Term Wins

"Win enough small battles early and when the larger ones come later they will seem small. Win enough larger ones and victory will be yours." (Dave Tantillo)

Tuesday morning could not come quick enough for me. We couldn't wait to see what we were going to compete in and what we would learn today. We were really feeling good about yesterday's victory, but we all knew this was another day and that we still had to bring our "A" game. We were all grounded in the fact that as a team we performed well, but on an individual basis *Team Delta Force* could crush us in any competitive event on any given day. We would soon discover our next event because Dr. B. came jogging onto the track.

"I guess most of you have figured out the type of event you will be competing in today. It has to do with running. To be exact, it has to do with long distance running. Today's competitive event is truly about teamwork and pacing yourself. Each team member will run, or for some, walk two miles in a relay-type format.

To be fair, male members will run against male members and female members will run against female members. You'll alternate genders each time you hand the baton off at the two-mile mark. The first female on each team will start the relay race with the last male on each team ending the race. It's the job of the team leader to decide who will be running each leg of the race," Dr. B. explained.

He continued, by saying, "My hope is through this event everyone will learn the seventh step of how to be a good leader. As usual, I will need the name of each of your team leaders. You have all morning to stretch out, practice, and devise your strategy of who will run each leg of the race. Good luck and I'll see you at 1:00," Dr. B. said. He turned around and jogged off of the track.

As soon as Dr. B. disappeared, we all immediately looked at Chris. We knew he was the fastest on our team because he clearly demonstrated this skill when he zipped past *Team Delta Force* while playing Capture the Flag. Plus, he hadn't been a team leader yet. He knew his time to lead was now and he wasted no time in stepping up to the plate.

"O.K., listen up, everyone. This is my event. I'll take the lead on this one. This isn't going to be easy for some of you guys, but I think I have a sound plan that may give us a chance to win," Chris said with a confident voice.

"Are you going to supply us with oxygen masks after most of us collapse after the first mile!" Isabella said in a joking way.

Chris was a rather thin person who stood about five foot ten. He was an African American with dreadlocks and hazel-green eyes. He was perceived initially as a very serious person who rarely cracked a smile. Chris seemed though he was always on the go and didn't have the time to smile or to stop and smell the roses. I couldn't figure out if he just naturally had a lot of energy to expend or if he suffered from Attention Deficit Hyperactivity Disorder. He just couldn't sit still!

"You'll be fine. Remember, Dr. B. said you could run the two miles or walk it," Chris replied to Isabella.

"If any of us walk the two miles, we'll have no chance of winning this event," said Jacob.

I replied, by saying, "I don't know if I can even make it through the first mile, let alone two miles!"

"Everyone needs to relax. Let's hear Chris out before we all start to panic. He said he has a plan. Go ahead Chris. What's the plan?" Jill asked quickly to prevent anyone else from experiencing another panic attack.

"We have a lot of work ahead of us, so I'm going to talk fast!" Chris said anxiously.

Jill immediately jumped in again, by saying, "Chris...remember what Dr. B. said yesterday? Rome wasn't built in one day, so you need to slow down a little bit in explaining your plan. Give us some time to catch our breath and absorb what you're going to ask us to do this afternoon."

"Sorry. Sometimes I don't realize when to stop or slow down. Thanks Jill for keeping me in check," Chris said apologetically.

"No problem Chris," Jill said.

Chris continued again, by saying, "Let's start over this time, but at a slower pace. When the race begins..."

When 1:00 came, our spirits were running pretty high. Chris laid out a sound plan for us, but it all depended upon how far our legs would carry us. Dr. B. sprinted onto the track this time instead of jogging like this morning. Maybe he just ate a big bowl of Wheaties!

"Hey Dr. B., how come you sprinted this time onto the track?" Jacob asked.

"Sometimes you have to know when to jog and when to sprint if you want to become a good leader, but that isn't step seven," Dr. B. said, as he was trying to catch his breathe.

"So, whose our two team leaders today?" asked Dr. B.

"I will be the team leader for *Team Delta Force*," said Logan.

"And, why may I ask?" asked Dr. B.

"Well, my name Logan was given to me by my parents because they both loved this movie at the time called 'Logan's Run'. In the movie, Logan ran a lot, so I took up running at a young age and I can proudly say that I am an All-American sprinter for my high school. I guess running is in my blood and in my name," Logan replied with a very confident tone.

"Very good analogy, Logan! Now let's hear from *Team L.O.T.*," said Dr. B.

"I'm going to be the team leader today Dr. B.," said Chris.

"Once again, and why?" asked Dr. B.

"I guess because I have been running my whole life, but not for any school. I have been running back and forth to school since first grade.

I believe I can best lead my team to victory because of my running experience," Chris said.

"I don't think running back and forth to school qualifies you as a good runner. Now being an All-American sprinter is a great credential for being a good runner!" Logan said, as he and the rest of *Team Delta Force* were laughing at Chris.

"You shouldn't poke fun at people until you've walked in their shoes!" Chris said with an angry voice.

"Or in your case Chris, until you 'so call run' in the other person's shoes!" Logan sarcastically replied.

"Stop it right now, Logan! I've warned your team for the last time about the sarcastic remarks. The next person who makes a sarcastic remark will sit out that day's event. You'll have to play one man down for that event. So, let's set the order. Who's racing against who?" Dr. B. asked. The line-up for the team relay race was as follows:

Team LOT	vs	**Team Delta Force**
Emily	vs	Brittney
Dave	vs	Jackson
Olivia	vs	Jessica
Ben	vs	Alex
Isabella	vs	Angelina
Jaden	vs	Adam
Grace	vs	Brooke
Jacob	vs	Trevor
Jill	vs	Destiny
Chris	vs	Logan

"Everybody, huddle up! Remember the plan. Remember our lives depend on winning!" Chris said with a serious tone.

After we broke the huddle, we all went to our respective positions on the track to await Dr. B.'s whistle. Before I could even take a deep breathe, Dr. B. blew his whistle. The relay race had begun!

As suspected, *Team Delta Force* took a commanding lead. Brittney finished the first relay twenty feet ahead of Emily. I was next. I didn't beat Jackson, but I was able to close the gap with *Team Delta Force* by two more feet. This trend of closing the gap continued as the baton was passed onto Olivia, then Ben, then Isabella, then Jaden, then Grace, then Jacob, and then Jill. But, then something unexpected occurred when Jill was handing the baton off to Chris so he could run the final leg of the race.

"CRASH!" That was the sound of Jill and Chris colliding into each other on the final exchange of the baton. The next thing we saw was a big cloud of dirt caused by the collision. When the dust had settled, we saw Chris picking Jill up to make sure she was all right. Then, we saw Jill grab him by his collar and look him straight in the face with a mean look and say something to him. I'm not sure what it was she said, but Chris took off like he had ants in his pants.

Meanwhile *Team Delta Force* had a commanding lead. Logan saw the collision in the corner of his eye, so he took off in a full out sprint. It appeared he wanted to stretch the lead, so he had a large enough cushion between him and Chris. After the first mile it appeared that there was no way we were going to win the game. Chris was at least an eighth of a mile behind Logan with only a mile to go. How is Chris going to beat an All-American sprinter?

As we were cheering and screaming at the top of our lungs, we noticed after each quarter mile, Chris was picking up some major ground. We weren't sure if Chris was picking up speed or if Logan was slowing down. When they both rounded the last quarter mile mark, they were dead even. We were jumping up and down and yelling for Chris to run for his life.

Chris was in full stride from the time he took off to start his leg of the race until he crossed the finished line. Logan on the other hand took off like a rocket in the beginning hoping he would gain enough lead that he could breeze through the finish line. Unfortunately for Logan, he appeared to lose his steam at the end of the race. Just as they approached the last twenty feet of the race, Logan started to slow up and Chris just glided past him to cross the finish line first. Chris's plan had worked!

"Unbelievable finish, Chris!" Dr. B. yelled, as he jogged up to the finish line to congratulate Chris.

"Thanks Dr. B.," Chris replied, as he was trying to catch his breath.

"I wasn't sure how you guys were going to pull this event off? *Team Delta Force* is composed of some good athletes and running two miles isn't an easy task. How did you do it?" asked Dr. B.

"It was Chris's game plan that won it for us!" Jill shouted with excitement, as she was hugging Chris.

"After you catch your breath Chris, I have to know how you pulled it off," Dr. B. asked with baited breath.

"I knew right off the bat Dr. B. that my team was going to be overwhelmed with the task of trying to run a team total of twenty miles, and run it faster than a group of athletes," Chris said.

"How did you calm them down?" asked Dr. B.

"I told my teammates not to think of the one long relay race, but to think about it as ten small races. Our job was to focus on completing one small race at a time," Chris replied.

"You're onto something big, Chris. Please continue," Dr. B. said.

"The next step was to teach everyone that you don't have to beat your opponent to put us in a position to win," Chris said.

"I'm a little confused, Chris. If you told everyone that they didn't have to beat their opponent, then how would you ever win?" Dr. B. asked.

Chris laughed at first, and then said, "I told my teammates they didn't have to beat their opponent, but I had to if we wanted to win the relay race."

"Very clever, Chris! Please continue," Dr. B. said.

"You see the strategy was to put me in a position where I could win the last leg of the race. The team goal was to keep pace with the opposing runner from *Team Delta Force* and not try to beat them. Each time we handed off the baton to the next person, we would try and close the gap. It looked like we were losing at every point in the race, but we were actually making short-term wins. Each hand-off we were making progress. We started the race being twenty feet behind *Team Delta Force*. By the time Jill handed the baton off to me, we were only five feet behind them. Then the collision happened!" Chris said with angst.

"What happened on the exchange Chris?" asked Dr. B.

"I don't know, but I was more concerned about Jill being hurt than winning the race. By the time I got up, I could see in the corner of my eye Logan in a full sprint trying to stretch the lead. For a brief moment, I didn't think I could win at this point, but that changed quickly because of what Jill said to me," Chris said with a smile on his face.

"And, what was that?" Dr. B. asked

"She grabbed my collar and said 'You better run for your life'!" Chris said.

"I'm confused again. Why would Jill want you to run for your life?" asked Dr. B.

"Probably because I told them that the only way we were going to stay pace with our opponent and close the gap is if we ran like we were running for our lives," Chris said.

"That's quite a motivating technique you used, but how were you able to beat Logan? He is an All-American sprinter, and he had quite a lead on you," Dr. B. said.

"It wasn't easy, but I knew two things were true. First, Logan is a sprinter and not a long distance runner. Remember we were running a marathon and not a sprint. I knew eventually after he sprinted the first quarter mile that eventually he would start losing ground on me. It just happened to be closer to the end than I expected," Chris said.

"What was the second thing?" asked Dr. B. "It was what I taught everyone on my team. Run for your life. What you, Logan, and the rest of *Team Delta Force* don't know is that I live in a bad part of town. I run back and forth to school everyday because I am running for my life. I don't want to get mugged, shot, or killed. To beat Logan, I had to imagine I was running home from school being chased by a thug who had a gun," Chris said.

"I guess if I had to imagine what you go through every day I could've won the race too," Dr. B. said with a concerned voice.

"You see Dr. B., the only way my teammates could stay pace against their opponents and create these short wins was by closing the gap. I had to convince them that they were running for their lives. I told them how I have to run for my life everyday. I beat Logan because he was running for his ego. I was running for my life," Chris said proudly.

"Well Chris you stumbled upon the seventh step of how to become a good leader and you taught me a valuable lesson along the way. The seventh step is called short-term wins. When leading a team on a long journey, or in your case a marathon, short-term wins are the best recipe for success.

First, each short-term win gives the team evidence that their hard work is paying off. Second, with each win comes positive feedback, which will build morale. Third, it will disprove all nay Sayers and shun any cynics. Fourth, each win will prove to upper management that you're on the right track and progress is being made. Finally, the most important thing short-term wins does is build momentum," Dr. B. said.

"So, our short-term wins were after each exchange of the baton. We could see our hard work was paying off because the gap was closing faster and faster with each handoff. We were basically building momentum without even knowing it. Right, Dr. B.?" asked Chris.

"Exactly, Chris!" Dr. B. said with a smile.

"So, how did I teach you a valuable lesson Dr. B.?" asked Chris.

"Well Chris, it's quite simple. Most people understand the concept that most great leaders will look death in the face. They're not afraid to die because the cause they are fighting for is bigger than they." Dr. B. said.

"I didn't look death in the face. I ran from it!" laughed Chris.

"That's the lesson you taught me, Chris. Sometimes great leaders can win the war by running from death. If you die in battle foolishly, then who'll win the war? Would you rather be a known as the leader who gave his life to win a battle, but eventually lost the war? Or, would you rather be known as the leader who lost one battle by retreating, but won the war because it was wiser to fight another day? You run from death back and forth to school everyday. Maybe you run because you are afraid to die, or maybe the Lord has bigger and better things for you…like today's relay race!" Dr. B. said with a smile.

"As for you, Logan, let me give you a little advice. Running for your life will always beat running for your ego every time. Maybe you should have watched the movie your parents named after you. The character named 'Logan' in the movie 'Logan's Run' was running for his life throughout the entire movie. Maybe if you had learned how to run for your life, you might have beaten Chris. Life is not a sprint. Life is a marathon. And, before you make fun of someone you don't know much about, maybe you should walk in his shoes first. Or, run in his shoes if you choose to pick on Chris again." Dr. B. said.

He continued, by saying, "Now for Wednesday, we will learn the eighth step of how to become a good leader. Here is your hint as to what you will be learning and what activity you will be performing. As a parent, sometimes you stand behind your child, so you can catch them when they fall down. Sometimes you stand next to them, so you can hold their hand when they are scared.

But, sometimes you have to stand in front of them to protect them from harm. There are people in life and in the business world who want to do you harm. Don't let them steal your pride, money or your breakfast food off your plate! See you guys tomorrow in the gym at 9 A.M.," Dr. B. said, as he turned and walked off the track. Everyone looked at each other and laughed at Dr. B.'s hint.

"Who would want to steal the breakfast off your plate?" asked Jacob.

"I would if I was hungry. Just kidding!" said Isabella.

"I think the phrase stealing breakfast food is a hint, so everyone go home tonight and come up with a list of breakfast foods. I think the other hint has to do with when we should stand up and protect what we believe in," Jill said.

I jumped into the conversation, and said "I agree with Jill about writing down all different types of breakfast foods. Tomorrow morning we'll try and figure out what activity we'll compete in."

Jill turned to me and gave me a smile because I supported her suggestion. I just blushed and smiled back. I can't wait for tomorrow to come. I need to run home and make my list.

Chapter Summary

- Step 7 in becoming a leader is the ability to generate "*Short-term Wins.*"
- There are five reasons why a good leader believes in generating short-term wins:
    1.) Each short-term win gives the team evidence that their hard work is paying off.
    2.) With each win comes positive feedback, which will build morale.
    3.) It will disprove all naysayers and shun any cynics.
    4.) Each win will prove to upper management that you're on the right track and progress is being made.
    5.) The most important thing short-term wins does is build momentum.
- A leader would rather be known as the one who lost one battle by retreating, but won the war instead of the one who gave his life to win one battle, but eventually lost the war.
- Running for your life will always beat running for your ego every time.
- Life is not a sprint. Life is a marathon.

Chapter 9
Hedging Yourself

"Love your neighbor—but don't pull down your hedge." (Benjamin Franklin)

We all had our lists in our hand, when we all met in the gym Wednesday morning. After listing about forty different breakfast food items, everyone pretty much gave up trying to figure out Dr. B.'s hint. I was quite impressed by Isabella's list because most people had five to ten items on their list. Isabella had thirty items. I guess she must love variety in her breakfast food. As Dr. B. walked into the gym, we decided to give up trying to guess because we'll know soon enough.

"Good morning everyone! Today you're going to learn the eighth step of how to become a good leader. To help you in your journey to discover this step, I'm going to let you sort of break the law!" Dr. B. said in a laughing way.

"What do you mean break the law?" asked Jill.

"Relax everyone. I am referring to the game you guys are going to play. It's called 'Steal the Bacon'. You're not going to really steal anything. I was using a figure of speech," Dr. B. said.

"Here's the bean bag you will be using. Or to be technical, here is the bacon you will be stealing. Have fun breaking the law and I'll be back at 1:00," Dr. B. said laughingly, as he headed through the gym doors.

Of course, everyone laughed at Dr. B.'s feeble attempt of making a joke that stealing the bacon is breaking the law. Our team was down to three people who could become a team leader. It was either going to be Isabella, Jacob, or myself. I was about to raise my hand for this event when Isabella immediately spoke.

"If it's O.K. with everyone, I would like to be the team leader today?" asked Isabella. I didn't want to create conflict, so I went along with everyone and voted her in.

Isabella was a very proud, Hispanic American young girl, who happened to be pleasantly plump. Literally! She had a very pleasant personality and was always filled with vigor. I use the term plump because I don't like the term fat or overweight. Isabella just happened to be around five foot two, but probably weighed over two hundred pounds. The best thing about Isabella is that she didn't let her physical appearance discourage her from sparking up a conversation with someone she didn't know.

When 1:00 arrived, Isabella immediately raised her and shouted to Dr. B. as he walked into the gym, "Dr. B...I will be *Team L.O.T.'s* leader this afternoon!" Like I said before, Isabella had no problem calling attention to her self.

"Well, Isabella, I commend you for stepping up and standing out in the crowd," Dr. B. said with a smile on his face.

He continued, "Why have you decided to lead your team today Isabella?"

"Well, Dr. B., I love to eat as you can see by my great figure!" Isabella jokingly said.

She went on, by saying, "Who better to steal the bacon, than the only person on my team who loves to eat, especially bacon!"

We all laughed on the team because we knew Olivia was joking; however, *Team Delta Force* refrained from laughing because they didn't want Dr. B. jumping down their throat like the other days.

"That's a novel way of thinking, Olivia. But, I have decided not to question your team's line of thinking when it comes to picking a team leader," Dr. B. said.

He then turned to *Team Delta Force* and asked them who their team leader was going to be. Angelina raised her hand, but gave no good reason other than the team voted her to lead today. *Team Delta Force* is either up to something no good or they have decided to check out of the competition early. I thought they were up to no good!

Dr. B. told us to go to our respective sides. We all sat down and Dr. B. assigned each of us a number. After assigning numbers to both teams, he walked to the centerline and placed the beanbag on the floor.

As soon as he backed away, he yelled, "Number one."

Jill bolted from our team and Alex sprinted from the other team. They both met at the center at the same time.

It was a stalemate for some time, so Dr. B. called out, "Number 10."

Emily from our team raced to the center, and Brittney from the other team soon joined the melee. No one was still able to steal the bacon.

So, Dr. B. yelled out, "Numbers two, three, four and five!"

Now things were getting real crowded, but gridlock occurred when Dr. B. sent numbers six, seven, eight, and nine to the scrum. I have a feeling things are about to get out of hand.

As predicted before the game, *Team Delta Force* was up to no good. Apparently, their game plan to win was to position some of their players behind some of our fastest players. Next, they would kneel down behind our fastest players. Then, someone else from their team would push our players from the front, knocking our players over on their butts. This would give *Team Delta Force* an unfair advantage for a short moment because they had more people standing on their feet in hopes they could steal the bacon.

Isabella caught onto their strategy, so she decided to counter their strategy with one of her own. As people were circling around the bacon, Isabella waddled up to each one of us and whispered her plan in our ears. When she had finished whispering to the last member of our team, she walked directly toward the bacon. The plan was when she got to the bacon and stopped, we would execute "Operation Pancake!"

When Isabella reached the bacon, she turned to us and gave us the nod. Immediately, the fastest people on our team (Chris, Ben, Jacob, and myself) formed a wall on one side of the center circle where the bacon was situated. As predicted, *Team Delta Force* sent their henchman to position themselves behind the four of us. When the time was right, the four behind us knelt down and another four members of *Team Delta Force* simultaneously pushed us from the front sending all four of us to the floor. The trap was set!

When Isabella saw this happen, she immediately bull rushed the four members of *Team Delta Force* who pushed us over. She literally pancaked all four of them with all her girth. With the four of us falling on top of the four *Team Delta Force* members who knelt behind us, and the four members now getting pancaked by Isabella, there were two *Team Delta Force* members left to our five members. It was Alex and Angelina versus Jill, Emily, Olivia, Grace and Jaden.

However, unbeknownst to Alex and Angelina, Emily and Grace had snuck behind them and knelt down while Isabella made her pancaking debut. Before Alex and Angelina had realized what was happening, Jill and Jaden bumped into them and sent them falling to the floor, just like they had been doing to us all game long. With no one left standing from *Team Delta Force*, Jill picked up the bacon and bolted to our side to win the game. The plan was executed to perfection! Dr. B. was laughing hysterically at what had just transpired.

"Just when I've seen it all, you guys go and pull off the most incredible ways to win a game," Dr. B. said, as he was trying to catch his breath because he was laughing so hard.

Team Delta Force didn't appreciate our plan or the fact Dr. B. was laughing at the situation. A pushing match started to occur between both teams.

"Enough!" Dr. B. screamed.

He blew his whistle so loud we all had to stop shoving each other to cover our ears to prevent our eardrums from popping.

"Let's ALL go to our mutual corners and calm down!" Dr. B. shouted.

He continued with a softer and even keeled tone of voice, and said, "What happened out there?"

"They cheated!" shouted Alex.

"You cheated first! We just decided to fight fire with fire!" shouted Jill.

"Alright, already! Let's hear from the team leaders," asked Dr. B. Immediately Dr. B. turned to Angelina. You could tell she was embarrassed to say anything.

"It was all Alex's idea Dr. B.! I didn't want to cheat, but I was overruled. I guess I failed being the team leader," Angelina said, as she was lowering her head to the ground in shame.

"Actually, Angelina, it takes a lot of courage to admit what you just said knowing your group may be mad at you. I am proud of you for being truthful and taking a stand. Being truthful is one of the best qualities a person should possess if she wants to become a good leader. So, Isabella, what's this I hear about your plan called 'Operation Pancake'?" asked Dr. B.

Isabella started to laugh at first, but she regained her composure and said, "We saw *Team Delta Force* cheating by pushing us over all the time, so I wanted to come up with a way that would lure them into continuing their bad behavior. This is when I came up with 'Operation Pancake.' While everyone on *Team Delta Force* was trying to steal the bacon or trying to knock us over, I whispered the game plan to everyone on my team."

Olivia continued, by saying, "The plan had three parts to it. The first part was for the four fastest people on our team to line up next to each other. We banked on the fact that *Team Delta Force* would follow suit and set our four players up for a fall. As predicted, they knocked our four over. This is where the 'Operation Pancake' comes in. I would bull rush the four guys who pushed our four guys and pancake them to the ground. I wanted to create a barrier between the four guys now beneath me, the four members of my team, and the four members of the other team who knelt down. The odds were now in our favor!"

"This is getting interesting Isabella. What about part two and three of your plan?" asked Dr. B.

"Well, part two happened almost simultaneously to part one. We expected Alex and Angelina to be caught off guard watching eight of their members being pinned down by my rather tiny physique!" Isabella laughingly said.

She continued, by saying, "Emily and Grace slithered behind Alex and Angelina, and knelt behind waiting for Jill and Jaden to deliver the final push. We wanted them to feel the same pain they were giving us all game. Plus, I knew that they would never see it coming. When they hit the ground, part three was for Jill to pick up the bacon and run to victory!"

"Although I am not one for cheating, I can appreciate why you felt you had to execute part two of your plan. However, I would like to discuss part one of your plan. I believe you stumbled upon step eight of how to become a good leader. You said that you wanted to create a barrier between your remaining players and the opposing eight players. Is that correct?" asked Dr. B.

"That's correct, Dr. B!" Isabella happily replied.

"Step eight is all about creating a barrier or what I call '*Hedging Yourself*'. In two previous steps, we talked about reinforcing the positive and creating short-term wins to build momentum. Sometimes there are barriers that will slow down momentum or even have it come to a screeching halt.

These barriers include, but are not limited to, upper management discouraging the actions aimed to deliver the vision, inflexible formal organizational structures, poor or lack of performance appraisal systems, unfair compensation systems that undermine efforts to continuously improve, and/or other personnel in the company who try to undermine the project because they feel threatened that you are moving in on their turf," Dr. B. said.

He continued, by saying, "The best way to tackle these barriers is to remove them if possible. When removal is impossible, the concept of '*Hedging Yourself*' should be applied. Sometimes as a leader, you have to create a hedge between your team and those forces, which want to prevent your team from succeeding.

As Protector of the team, a good leader must hedge or shield her team from some of the barriers previously mentioned. A good leader must maintain discipline to be able to handle all types of conflict, while motivating her team to remain focused on delivering the vision. This is where Isabella's 'Operation Pancake' comes into play.

You saw the conflict occurring Olivia, when you witnessed what *Team Delta Force* was doing to your teammates. By pancaking them, you created a barrier, so the rest of the team could deliver the vision. Or, in your case, steal the bacon, so your team could win!" Dr. B. said with a smile.

He continued by cautioning us, by saying, "Just remember to keep your Hedge manicured low, and not permanent. Keep it manicured low, so upper management can always look over the hedge and see the progress. Finally, don't keep your hedge permanent, because it will prevent you and your team from performing the ninth step of becoming a good leader."

Dr. B. paused for a moment, and then continued, by saying, "Tomorrow you will be competing in one of the ultimate team sports. It will require all the physical strength you possess. It will test your endurance. It will test your mind. It will test your ability to work together. If I were a betting man, I would put my money initially on *Team Delta Force* because they are more physically equipped to handle this event. However, by applying everything you have learned so far, *Team L.O.T.* does have an outside chance to win the event.

Here is a lengthy hint for you as to what you will be doing and learning tomorrow. If you don't take what you've learned so far and permanently anchor it within your team's culture, then you'll eventually be pulled back into the old way of doing things.

Remember, changing a culture takes patience, time, teamwork, and most of all faith in what you believe is right. When the time is right, you'll be able to pull those non-believers over to your side very easily because the non-believers are just too tired to fight anymore. Or, you didn't waver in your beliefs during a lengthy barrage of personal attacks. Or, they finally see the merits of accepting the change. Good luck and I'll see you all tomorrow in the track and field area."

As Dr. B. left the gym, my team looked at Jacob and I. We were the last two people left on the team who haven't led our team yet.

"That was a very long hint he gave us. I'm a little uneasy by the fact that he said *Team Delta Force* was more physically equipped than us," Jacob said with an unsettling voice.

"Maybe he's playing with our minds Jacob," Jill said to calm people's anxieties.

"And, if he isn't Jill?" asked Jacob.

"Then, let's take his advice of making sure we apply everything we've learned so far and compete tomorrow with our feet planted firmly on the ground and our heads held high," Jill said, as though she was making a halftime speech in a football game. Tomorrow will be interesting. I just hope I don't let everyone down if I'm the team leader tomorrow and we fail miserably.

Chapter Summary

- Step 8 in becoming a leader is the ability to *"Hedge Yourself."*
- Good leaders will always remove barriers that will slow down momentum or even have it come to a screeching halt.
- Sometimes as a good leader, you have to create a hedge between your team and those forces, which want to prevent your team from succeeding.
- A good leader must have the maintained discipline to be able to handle all types of conflict, while motivating her team to remain focused on delivering the vision.
- Keep your Hedge manicured low, and not permanent. Keep it manicured low, so upper management can always look over the hedge and see the progress. Don't keep your hedge permanent because it will prevent you and your team from performing the ninth step of becoming a good leader.

Chapter 10
Institutionalizing the Vision

"Institutionalizing a leadership-centered culture is the ultimate act of leadership." (John P. Kotter—author of *Leading Change*)

Thursday came too quick. I dreaded walking into the track and field area. When I finally made my way onto the field, I knew immediately what our team was in for today. Dr. B. was right in that it was one of the ultimate team sports and it would require physical strength. We we're going to compete with *Team Delta Force* in a game called "Tug of War". It might get real ugly for us this afternoon unless a miracle happens! Dr. B. walked onto the track and field area with a big smile on his face.

"I'm sure by now everyone has figured out what event you'll be practicing for this afternoon. It is the classic game of 'Tug of War'. The goal is to pull the rope until the center red flag crosses over your team's white line. The match is best out of three. So, buckle up, it may be a long afternoon. Or, maybe not!" Dr. B. said as he was looking at us when he made the last statement. He then walked off the field and didn't return until 1:00.

Jacob was miffed at Dr. B.'s innuendo about how it might be a short afternoon because we probably will lose the match.

"I want to be the team leader on this event!" Jacob said with anger in his voice.

"Let's build on Jacob's passion to prove Dr. B. wrong. I nominate Jacob to lead us in this event," Jill said.

We all agreed Jacob would lead us in the event, but I hope he doesn't let his anger cloud his ability to lead us. Before I could finish my thought, Jacob said the most bizarre thing.

He said, "I'll be back in a while, I have to go do something right now. Start stretching out and I'll be back as soon as I can." With that, he took off and headed towards the high school.

Jacob was the type of person you probably didn't want to tick off. Although he stood around six foot tall, he was quite wide. He was your prototypical farm boy. Jacob was very stocky and probably weighed close to four hundred pounds if not more. He either wore overalls and a flannel shirt when we were outside or carpenter shorts with a pocket t-shirt when we were inside. He's the only person I know who could play sports in his work boots. Jacob was a gentle giant all in all, but I sure didn't want to be the one to tick him off. He could crush anyone with his bare farm hands if he really wanted too! About two hours went by before Jacob returned back to the track and field area.

"I'm sorry about leaving you guys for two hours, but it was real important for me to step away if we're going to have any chance of winning this afternoon," Jacob said sincerely.

"Where did you wander off to?" asked Jill.

Jacob immediately replied, by saying, "I'll tell you in a moment, but listen closely to what I'm about to say because I have a plan that will help us win this afternoon. The first thing we have to do is…"

There was so much testosterone flying around when Dr. B. arrived at 1:00 we could have bottled it up, sold it at a nutrition store, and made millions. Both teams were determined to win the match.

We all had our game faces on when Dr. B. turned to us, and said, "You better have brought your "A" game because you're going to need it this afternoon to beat *Team Delta Force!*"

Jacob immediately snapped back at Dr. B. saying, "Before you ask, let me save you some time. I'm *Team L.O.T. 's* leader today. Before you ask why, let me tell you because I want to prove to you that our team does have a chance to win even if you think we're not physically equipped to do so!

"My, my, Jacob! I sense you aren't happy with my earlier comments. First of all, they weren't supposed to be derogatory. It was only an observation, but I love to be proven wrong," Dr. B. said with a smile on his face.

"I'm going to be the leader for *Team Delta Force* Dr. B.," said Trevor.

"And, did you volunteer like Jacob or were you nominated. It was a combination of both. The team nominated me, but I also wanted to be the team leader anyway due to the fact I'm probably the strongest member on the team. I'm also the captain of the school wrestling team. I wrestle in the heaviest weight class, so I probably would be a good anchor person for my team," Trevor said confidently.

"Makes logical sense," said Dr. B.

He continued, by saying, "Well, apparently it appears that both teams are ready to battle it out today, so let's take our positions. The match is best out of three. I will blow my whistle to start the first game."

Dr. B. walked over to the center of the "Tug of War" playing area. We took our positions. Dr. B. raised his right hand in the air. He took his left hand and placed the whistle in his mouth.

Dr. B. started, by saying, "Ready. Set. Go!"

By the time Dr. B. had finished blowing his whistle, *Team Delta Force* had successfully dragged our team and the center red flag over their white line within thirty seconds. *Team Delta Force* was jumping for joy and high-fiving everyone because they literally knocked the wind out of our sails, and all the testosterone built-up inside us.

Dr. B. turned to us and didn't say a word. Based on his previous comments, I would've bet a sarcastic remark was coming. Instead, his face actually showed sadness as though he was feeling bad for our loss or disappointed we didn't prove him wrong.

He must have noticed we were reading his sad facial expression because immediately he became serious, and blurted out, "O.K. it's one to nothing. Let's line up for the second game!"

I'm not sure what Dr. B.'s up to, but I'm a little confused right now. Is he pulling for us to win or is he pulling for *Team Delta Force* to win. First it was sarcastic remarks to us and now it is sad looks because we failed the first time. We'll I'm sure we'll see that sad look again thirty seconds after he blows his whistle to start game two. I have a feeling game one is going to end up like game two.

"On your mark. Get set. Go!" Dr. B. said right before he blew his whistle for the second time.

This time the game was a little different. Thirty seconds went by and we were still in the game pulling with all our might. I thought to myself that we might actually have a chance to win. Jacob's plan was really working. Then, before I knew it, I went flying backwards landing on my butt with the rest of the butts on our team following suit. Did we just win this game?

As I looked, *Team Delta Force* was on ground laughing hysterically. Apparently, they thought it would be funny if they just let go of their grip all at once, so we could fall on the ground and look stupid. I guess they were so confident about beating us in the third game that they could afford to lose game two if it meant total embarrassment to our team. Then, the real Dr. B. finally appeared again.

"That was uncalled for *Team Delta Force*! Someone could've got hurt by you guys letting go of the rope," Dr. B. said angrily.

"The rope slipped out of our hands by mistake. Plus, the only thing that got hurt was their pride!" Alex said, as he was trying to hold back his laughter.

"We just wanted to keep the match more interesting, so we let them beat us this time. We had to let the farm boy and his hired hands win at least one game!" Trevor added.

"Keep your sarcasm to yourself Trevor and let's line up for the third and final game of the match," Dr. B. shouted.

As we were getting ready, Dr. B. turned to us and said quietly so *Team Delta Force* couldn't hear him, "Remember everything you learned these past two weeks. Remember also this is a team sport. United you'll stand. Divided you'll fall. Think positive thoughts. It will breed positive results. Good luck!"

As Dr. B. resumed his position in the center area, his face changed back to his angry face he had after *Team Delta Force* pulled their prank on us.

"Alright, this is for the match. Everyone take your positions," Dr. B. shouted.

For a brief moment, I could literally hear everyone's heartbeat racing on my team. Was it due to nervousness because we may lose? Was it due to anxiousness because we actually have a chance to win? I guess we'll know in a second.

"On your mark. Get set. Go!" Dr. B. said, as he blew his whistle.

The rope tightened up quickly. The red flag slowly started to move towards *Team Delta Force's* white line. At first glance, it would appear to anyone looking on that *Team Delta Force* was moments away from victory when their progress came to an abrupt halt. The red flag stopped one foot from their white line and hung there for the next thirty minutes. Then, something bizarre started to happen. Little by little, the red flag started to inch back towards *Team L.O.T.'s* side.

As I looked down the line of my teammates, I could see all of us working in unison. We had Jacob's plan, and we were going to live or die by it. At first his plan didn't look good, but eventually his plan really started to work. The red flag was now on our side. Little by little, the red flag inched toward our white line. The red flag apparently came to a halt again one foot from our white line. Another ten minutes had gone by and it looked like everyone on our team were losing their strength and their grip on the rope. We needed a miracle fast and I'm not sure where it was going to come from.

Before I finished my thought, the next thing I felt was the same feeling when someone kicks the legs out from beneath you. When I got up, I couldn't believe my eyes. The red flag had crossed our line and everyone on *Team Delta Force* was on the ground shaking their heads like there were cobwebs in them. We just won the match and I have no idea how we won. Dr. B. came running over and congratulated us on a tremendously executed victory.

"That was just pure incredible!' Dr. B. shouted.

He continued, "I really thought you guys gave up in the beginning, but you fought back and stuck with your game plan. Please tell me Jacob how you guys were able to overcome your minor setback and achieve the impossible?"

"Everything you saw was planned. From the time we were losing until the time we won. There was one part I neglected to tell my teammates, but I'll share that with you in a second," Jacob said with a smile on his face.

"You're trying to tell me that this was all choreographed by your team?" Dr. B asked in disbelief.

Jacob replied, "Yep. It all started this morning. This morning, I broke away from my team for two hours. I went straight to the school library and jumped onto the Internet to look up the rules and strategies of 'Tug of War'."

"That's brilliant, Jacob! Now that is true leadership!" Dr. B. exclaimed.

Jacob continued, by saying, "I had *Looked fear in the face* and *Envisioned* what we had to do to win. I *Assembled the team* by placing everyone in the right position. There are three positions on a 'Tug of War' squad. The frontmen are the lightest who were Jill, Emily, Grace, and Chris. The middlemen are the next heaviest who were Jaden, Dave, Olivia, Ben, and Isabella. The anchorman is the heaviest person on the squad, which is obviously myself.

Next, we *Discussed* the game plan. We would let *Team Delta Force* gain a lead and have them expound as much energy as possible initially, but keep in mind we still had to hold our ground. We were able to withstand their initial assault thank God, and that's why the red flag stopped close to their white line. After thirty minutes of withstanding *Team Delta Force's* attempts to win, I felt it was time to let *Empowerment* kick in. Everyone had a specific job to do. We all had to trust one another. We would all execute the team game plan together and in unison."

"What specific jobs are you referring to Jacob?" asked Dr. B.

"First, there was the job of the frontmen. They're the lightest on the team. Their job is to pull hard and fast with the hope of making the other team lose their grip. Next, there was the job of the middlemen. They're the middleweight people on the team. Their job is to pull the rope inch-by-inch as the frontmen work hard to make the other team lose their grip on the rope," Jacob said.

"I assume you're the anchorman?" Dr. B. asked with a smile.

"Yes I am! The job of the anchorman is to hold the rope taunt and at a level, so all his players are able to wrap their arm around the rope and establish a good grip throughout the entire match. Plus, the anchorman should be the heaviest person on the team because you want to have your opponent try and drag the most weight from the furthest distance. My job is to anchor myself and be the dead weight for my team," Jacob replied.

"Where and when did *Empowerment* kick in?" asked Dr. B.

"Like I said, when thirty minutes had passed by, I felt it was time for all of us to execute our specific jobs together and in unison. Over the next ten minutes or so, we were *Reinforcing* each other with positive comments because it was taking a toll on us physically to regain the length of rope we gave up initially. We knew with each inch we pulled, we were making *Short-term gains*. We knew if we continued at this pace, the short-term gains would turn into a long-term win. But, when we got within one foot of our white line, our team had expounded so much energy we didn't have enough to close that one foot gap," Jacob said with a concerned voice.

"I noticed your team hung there for a brief moment. With very little energy left in your teammates, how the heck where you guys able to yank *Team Delta Force* to the ground and win the game?" asked Dr. B.

"Simple, Dr. B. I just applied the last step you taught us yesterday. I *hedged myself*!" Jacob said proudly.

"You hedged yourself? How did you do that?" asked Dr. B.

"Well, when I looked up the rules of 'Tug of War' this morning, I also looked up the definition of the word *hedge*. I found one definition of the word *hedge* I liked. It defined *hedge* as a means of protection or defense against loss. So, I came up with a contingency plan to defend my team's honor in the event we were losing or were about to lose," Jacob said.

"Pardon me, Jacob. So, I can understand, let me play back what I heard you just say to me. Metaphorically speaking, your contingency plan represented the *hedge* between winning and losing. Thus, you would only *hedge yourself* or use your contingency plan in the event you might lose. Is this correct?" Dr. B. asked.

"Yep!" said Jacob.

"So, I'm assuming you must have *hedged yourself* or basically you put your contingency plan into action because you ended up winning the game? Is this correct?" Dr. B. asked curiously.

Everyone on our team look a little puzzled while Jacob was talking to Dr. B. I wasn't sure what Jacob was talking about because he never discussed with us about a contingency plan. I had to ask Jacob the burning question.

"What are you talking about Jacob? We never talked about a contingency plan. What's up?" Dr. B. looked a little shocked that I didn't know what Jacob was talking about.

"My contingency plan was to make sure I didn't use up all my strength in the beginning. So, for the first forty minutes of the game, I basically used my weight and leverage to keep my team in the game. After forty minutes had expired, I noticed my team was getting tired and they needed one more *short-term win* to bring home the victory. It was then I finally used my strength. With all my weight, strength, and leverage, I tugged the rope so hard it sent both teams to the ground. When I looked up, the flag had crossed our white line and we won the game! I was wrong for not telling all of you. I'm truly sorry about that," Jacob said, as he turned his face to the ground in shame.

"That's O.K. Jacob. I accept your apology because your heart was in the right place. Next time tell us everything, not just on a need to know basis!" Jill said with a smile, as she tried to reach up and grab Jacob's shoulders on her tippy toes.

"It worked for you today, Jacob, but sometimes withholding information can backfire. Remember, a good leader doesn't tell half-truths. He tells the whole truth!" Dr. B. said.

Dr. B. Continued, by saying, "Well Jacob, I must say you have truly demonstrated today to me that you understand the ninth step of how to become a good leader. It's called *Institutionalize the Vision*. The ultimate act of a leader is when he is able to *Institutionalize* his vision. What I mean by this is a good leader will find a way to weave new practices into the current fabric of the culture. These new practices will now be visible to all, shared by all, and become deeply ingrained in the culture where they naturally become common practice. You demonstrated to me how you applied all the steps of how to become a good leader today."

"I did?" asked Jacob.

"Yes, but the best part is that you showed me that all the steps I taught you came naturally to you when you competed today. You have *Institutionalized* all eight previous steps you have learned over the past two weeks and woven them into your behavior. I am very proud of you, but there is one more step you and everybody else needs to learn before you go off and apply what you've learned to become good leaders," Dr. B. stated.

Dr. B. continued, by saying, "Tomorrow is our last day of Leadership Camp. It represents a culmination of everything you have learned over the past two weeks. We will have our last competitive event in the morning and then an awards ceremony in the afternoon. Here is a hint as to what you will learn and do tomorrow. Good leaders have the ability to take jumbled words that make no sense and line them up in a way that will transform the words into a vision embraced by this generation and passed onto the next generation. You'll need your thinking hats tomorrow. I'll see you in the school library at 9 A.M." Dr. B. turned and walked off the track and field area.

After Dr. B. left, we were all giving each other high five's and hugs because of our victory. We each told Jacob that we weren't mad at him because if we were in the same shoes as him we probably would have done the same thing. I couldn't believe tomorrow was our last day of camp. Oh no! I almost forgot. I'm going to be the team leader tomorrow. I hope I don't ruin our perfect record. What will everyone think of me if I fail? I'm not going to sleep well tonight. I can feel it!

Chapter Summary

- Step 9 in becoming a leader is the ability to "*Institutionalize the Vision.*"
- The ultimate act of a leader is when he is able to *Institutionalize* his vision. A good leader will find a way to weave new practices into the

current fabric of the culture. These new practices will now be visible to all, shared by all, and become deeply ingrained in the culture where they naturally become common practice.

- A good leader doesn't tell half-truths. He tells the whole truth!

Chapter 11
Produce New Leaders

"Leaders don't create followers, they create more leaders." (Tom Peters)

Friday morning came a little too quickly for me. My heart was pounding as I walked through the library doors. My whole team was sitting down around two tables. As I walked up to the tables, I could tell Jill was about to say something to me.

"Hey Dave. I really look forward to you leading us to a perfect record!" Jill said with a warm smile.

I paused for a moment because I was a little embarrassed and caught off guard by her compliment.

I replied to Jill, by saying, "I'll try to lead us to victory today, but I'm not sure what we'll be doing today. Plus, I don't think I can top Jacob's performance from yesterday."

As soon as I complimented Jacob, all eyes turned to him and off me. They started congratulating Jacob again for yesterday's win. I temporarily took the pressure off me and redirected the attention onto Jacob. That lasted for about a minute because Dr. B. then walked into the room.

"Good morning everyone! Today is going to be a little different from the other days. Our competition will occur this morning in a few minutes. By the way, the ceremony will be in the afternoon. You'll have no time to practice, so you better put your thinking caps on quickly. Who are our last two guinea pigs today?" Dr. B. asked. Of course, he already knew the answer.

"I'm the leader for my team," Jackson said.

I followed up, by saying, "And, I'll be the leader for *Team L.O.T.*"

All eyes were again looking at me. I just tried to tune them out and focus my attention on what Dr. B. was about to say next.

"Like I said yesterday afternoon, when I gave you a hint, a good leader has the ability to take jumbled words that make no sense and line them up in a way that will transform the words into a vision embraced by this generation and passed onto the next generation. Today you'll literally be jumbling words. Has anyone done a Jumble® before?" Dr. B. asked. Everyone on both teams raised their hand.

"To learn the tenth step of how to become a good leader, it will not require you to use all nine previous steps. It will require all of you to use your mind. I am going to pass out a Jumble® to both teams. The final word to the Jumble® is the tenth step of how to become a good leader. To make it a little more difficult, I gave you eight-letter words to unscramble. Does that sound easy so far?" Dr. B. asked. Everyone on both teams nodded in agreement.

"Now, you know I'm not going to let you off the hook that easy. There's a hitch. The final word can only be unscrambled by each team leader without the help of any of their team members. The first team leader to bring me the final word correctly spelled will win today's final event," Dr. B. said.

Did he just say what I thought he said? Did I have to do the final word by myself? What happens if I choke or have a brain freeze? I didn't realize my panic was so obvious until I felt someone gently grab my hand and touch my shoulder. It was Jill.

"Relax. You'll be great. Just focus on what he said about passing the vision on to the next generation and the clue at the bottom of the Jumble®," whispered Jill.

Immediately I felt a sudden calmness and peacefulness in my mind and soul. Jill's positive comments had calmed me down. All right, I need to focus right now.

"Here is a copy of the Jumble® for everyone. I will repeat this again. You can work as a team on the first six words, but only the team leader can work on the final word," Dr. B. said with a stern tone of voice. The Jumble® looked like this:

It is the Hallmark of every good leader!

"I'll give all of you until 11:00 to complete the Jumble®. If it goes pass 11:00, I'll give each team leader all six unscrambled words first. Then, I'll start giving both team leaders one clue at a time every five minutes until one team leader finally solves the final word. Any questions?" asked Dr. B. No one said a word.

"Then let's begin!" Dr. B. shouted.

As everyone on my team buried his or her head trying to solve the first six words, I had to come up with a strategy to win the game. Jill told me to remember his hint and look at the clue at the bottom by the final word. First, Dr. B.'s hint talked about "*passing on the vision to the next generation.*" Next, I have to read the clue at the bottom of the Jumble®. So, I looked at the bottom and the clue read, "*It is the Hallmark of every good leader.*" Now I have to figure out two things. What would a leader want to pass on to the next generation? And, what the heck does the word Hallmark mean?

As I looked up, I started scanning the library with the hope I could find the answer to both of these questions floating somewhere in the air. Then, something caught my eye. A dictionary! I immediately ran over and looked up the word Hallmark. The dictionary defined Hallmark as a mark indicating quality or excellence and it also means a distinctive characteristic or attribute. Before I could close the dictionary, Jaden came running over to me.

"Here! We solved the first word. It's MOTIVATE!" Jaden whispered to me.

I immediately filled in the first word. We only have five more words to go before I can start working on the final word. Now where was I again? Oh yeah, the word Hallmark. If I take the definition of Hallmark and reword the final clue at the bottom of the Jumble®, I might come up with another clue. I reworded the final clue now to say, "It is a distinctive characteristic or a mark of excellence of every good leader." I started to ponder again when…

"Dave! We have the next two words. They're TENACITY and TRUTHFUL!" Olivia whispered into my ear.

I then filled in the next two words. We're halfway there I thought. Now, getting back to the revised final clue. What would a good leader consider to be a distinctive characteristic? Well, some characteristics that come to mind are honesty, integrity, self-confidence…

"Over here!" Jacob tried to say in a non-conspicuous tone of voice.

I looked over and he was waving me over to my team, who were all sitting together working diligently to solve the other unscrambled words. As I was approaching them, Jacob ran up and met me halfway.

"We just figured out the fourth and fifth word. They're EMPOWERS and DECISIVE!" Jacob said with excitement.

I turned around and ran back to my seat and penciled in the two words. All right, I said to myself. We only have one word to go before its show time for me.

Now, getting back to that distinctive characteristics question. Am I missing something here? Then, it hit me. The distinctive characteristic definition of Hallmark was referring to the six words we needed to solve to get to the final word. So far, we have Motivate, Tenacity, Truthful, Empowers, and Decisive. That means the second definition of Hallmark must relate to the final clue. Let's see. The second definition defines Hallmark as a mark of excellence of every good leader. Now, what would a good leader consider to be a mark of excellence? Better yet, what would a good leader be most proud of at the end of the day?

Before I could finish my thought, I felt a warm hand touch my shoulder while I was sitting at my table. When I turned to see who it was, I became face to face with the one whom I admired these past two weeks. Yep! It was Jill.

She leaned towards me and gently whispered in my ear, saying, "I have the last word for you. It's INVOLVED! Now bring us home a victory. And, here's a little something to wish you good luck!" Jill leaned closer and gave me a little kiss on my cheek.

Wow! I all of a sudden became extremely motivated at this point. After she kissed my cheek, she walked away and went back to the group. I looked up to see if anyone saw, so I could brag about Jill kissing me but apparently no one was looking. Oh well! At least I know she kissed me. I need to focus now. It was 10:45 and I wanted to finish before 11:00 because I didn't want *Team Delta Force* to get a hint from Dr. B. to help them solve the final word.

With all six words unscrambled, I now can take all the letters from each word that were circled and try to rearrange them to solve the final word. Here is the list of six words:

```
T A M I V O E T
M O T I V A T E
A N T T I Y C E
T E N A C I T Y
L R T U H F T U
T R U T H F U L
M R O P S E W E
E M P O W E R S
E D S E V I I C
D E C I S I V E
V V L I O D E N
I N V O L V E D
```

By taking all the circled letters out, I came up with a list of the following letters:

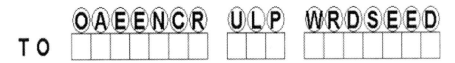

Now with all these letters and the clue about the word Hallmark being defined as a mark of excellence of every good leader, I should be able to solve the final word. The clock said 10:55 now! I can't panic. I need to think quickly.

Just then I remembered Dr. B.'s hint about *"passing the vision onto the next generation."* I guess if I were a leader, I would be proud to pass on my vision to the next generation or the next person who would be leading the vision. That's it! One of the words has to be leader or leaders. I'll see if there is a six or seven letter word and I'll fill it in.

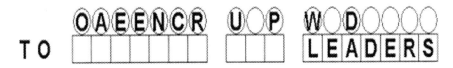

Alright! The word "Leaders" seems to fit, so now what are the other two words? It's 10:57! Keep thinking.

Well, if the Hallmark or true measure of a good leader is to pass it onto the next generation, then they have to make sure the new leaders are trained properly to carry on the vision. That's it! I think the middle word is "NEW"!

Oh no it's 10:59! I have one minute left to try and figure out the last word. I looked over to my team and they were all staring at me. They were all fidgety because Jackson from *Team Delta Force* was also working on the final word and he was now gesturing to Dr. B. to come over and look at his final word. It's too late. I probably lost because Dr. B. was looking at Jackson's answer. I just looked down at my table in sheer disappointment.

Then it happened again, I felt a warm gentle tap my shoulder. It was Jill again. She leaned toward my right ear, whispering, "Don't give up on me right now! Dr. B. just shook his head to Jackson indicating he had the wrong answer. You can do it. Just relax. The next thing you know it, you'll be producing some new ideas to solve the last word. Good luck." Then, Jill walked away.

Jill's positive comments relaxed me for the moment, but the clock was about to strike 11:00 and I haven't produced any new ideas yet to solve that darn final clue. The only thing I was about to produce was failure. Good leaders would never produce failure. They would only produce good leaders. That's it! PRODUCE! The Hallmark of any good leader is the ability "To Produce New Leaders!" I used the remaining letters to fill in the last word and guess what?

I think I did it! Dr. B. was about to give us our first clue, when I interrupted him and asked him to come over and look at my answer. He walked over, picked up my sheet, and studied it for eternity. It seemed like eternity, but later everyone told me it was only about ten seconds.

He then handed it back to me and with a serious look on his face, he said, "I saw your facial expression when I walked over to Jackson. I could tell you felt defeated. However, I am also proud of you for not giving up because you just solved the final word and have led your team to their final victory!"

Our team went ballistic in the library when they heard what Dr. B. had said to me. We were jumping up and down and hugging each other with sheer excitement. I even hugged Jill twice. I did say to her on our second hug it was her last comment to me that helped me solve the last word.

I thanked her profusely for her help, her kind reassuring words, and her warm, gentle touch. I think I saw her blush for the first time when I showered her with all the compliments. What a way to finish the week. Our team went undefeated and I led our team to its final victory. Two weeks I'll never forget.

"O.K., listen up, everyone. I know your excited *Team L.O.T.*, but I need to share with everyone the tenth step of how to become a good leader," Dr. B. shouted, as he tried to talk over our noisy team's excitement.

He continued, "The Hallmark of becoming a good leader is to develop strong subordinates who will eventually become your successor or somebody else's successor in the company. Organizations can ill afford to be led by only a few leaders. They need to make an investment in potential successors. They need to *produce new leaders*, which is the tenth step."

"How does an organization *produce new leaders?*" asked Jill.

"Great question, Jill! There is no sure method, but let me offer one blueprint an organization could follow to *produce new leaders*. First, the organization's upper management needs to buy into the concept of succession planning. Second, they need to recruit from the outside or to identify internally candidates who have leadership potential. Third, assign a senior level mentor to each potential candidate," Dr. B. said with a sarcastic smile.

"How come you're smiling funny Dr. B.?" asked Jill.

"If an organization can get past these first three steps, (which tend to be the hardest for any organization) then the rest of the steps seem to flow effortlessly. The fourth thing an organization needs to do is to create a career plan for each candidate to expose each individual to as many different aspects of the company.

The purpose of several lateral positions is to help each candidate develop a wide range of leadership skills in different areas of the organization, teach him or her the difficulties of leadership, teach him or her how difficult it is to produce change, and help create an informal personal network inside and outside of the work environment. Finally, the fifth thing organizations need to do is to produce new leaders and actually place them in a leadership position when their career plan has been fulfilled," said Dr. B.

"Those aren't five easy things to do Dr. B.!" said Jill.

"You're absolutely correct, Jill! But, that's what separates the well-led organizations who will survive many years down the road from those poorly-led organizations who are here today and gone tomorrow. If an organization wants to be around tomorrow, then it needs to produce new leaders today so they can pass on the founder's original vision and not forget why they are in business in the first place. This is why the slogan for Leadership Camp is called *Teaching Tomorrow's Leaders Today!*" Dr. B. said.

"I apologize for interrupting, but how are we ever going to memorize all ten steps of how to become a good leader let alone the blueprint to produce new leaders," I asked.

Dr. B. replied, by saying, "The blueprint is important, but that is more of a choice for an organization or a group of senior managers to know, embrace, and implement. Let's just focus on the ten steps because they apply more to you and I. There is a simple way to remember all ten steps. If you take the first letter of each first word of each step, you'll spell one word. Can anyone guess what that ten-letter word would be if you take the first ten letters?"

Everyone started to write down all ten steps furiously on paper. Let's see. Step one is...

Look Fear in the Face—Step 1
Envision the Vision—Step 2
Assemble the Team—Step 3
Discuss the Vision—Step 4
Empower the Team—Step 5
Reinforce the Positive—Step 6
Short-term Wins—Step 7
Hedging Yourself—Step 8
Institutionalize the Vision—Step 9
Produce New Leaders—Step 10

"Wow Dr. B.! Will you look at that! The ten steps spell leadership!" I said.

"Good job Dave! I have used the word 'Leadership' as an acronym to represent all ten steps of how to become a good leader. You'll probably forget about this camp and me in ten years, but I'll bet you'll never forget about my 'Leadership Acronym'!" Dr. B. said with a happy, yet somewhat sad smile.

"We'll never forget about you!" everyone said in unison from *Team L.O.T.*

Team Delta Force just sat there quiet because they were still sulking about losing all ten events to a bunch of misfits.

"So, Dr. B., what's going on this afternoon? You said something about an award ceremony?" I asked with great curiosity.

Dr. B. replied, by saying, "I'll be giving out one award this afternoon to the individual that has truly exemplified what it takes to be a good leader. It will be someone who has learned all the steps along the way, but has also shown he or she could lead whether they were the team leader for that day or just a supporting team member. This individual will be given the honor and privilege of receiving the only award given out at Leadership Camp. It is called the *Young Leader of Tomorrow Award*. And, I can proudly tell you that I will be giving the award this afternoon to..."

Chapter Summary

- Step 10 in becoming a leader is the ability to "*Produce New Leaders.*"
- The Hallmark of becoming a good leader is to develop strong subordinates who will eventually become your successor or somebody else's successor in the company.
- Five steps an organization could follow to *produce new leaders* are:
  - 1.) Upper management needs to buy into the concept of succession planning.
  - 2.) Recruit from the outside or identify internally candidates who have leadership potential.

3.)   Assign a senior level mentor to each potential candidate.

4.)   Create a career plan for each candidate to expose each individual to as many different aspects of the company.

5.)   Place them in a leadership position when their career plan has been fulfilled.

- Candidates should train in several lateral positions to develop a wide range of skills.
- If an organization wants to be around tomorrow, then it needs to produce new leaders today so they can pass on the founder's original vision and not forget why they are in business in the first place.

Chapter 12
The Interview

As I finished writing the tenth step of how to become a good leader on my pad of paper, I was feeling a little better now about being able to ask some intelligent questions to this individual, who'll be applying for the new Director of Leadership position at my company. I called out to my assistant to ask her to have the candidate wait in my office when he arrives. I had to step out of my office for a minute I told her.

When I came back, I opened my office door and I noticed something odd. There was a woman standing with her back to me staring at the pictures on my shelf.

As I approached her, I asked, "Excuse me, but can I help you?"

She didn't turn around, but she did reply back to me, by saying, "After all these years, I can't believe you still have this picture sitting on your shelf."

I stopped dead in my tracks when I heard her response. I knew that voice, but I couldn't place the face. As I was struggling to figure out the voice, the woman then turned around and looked me dead in the eyes. The next thing I knew. I started going on an emotional roller coaster ride. First, I was in shock. Then, I was excited. Finally, I was embarrassed.

"Are you the candidate I'm supposed to interview today?" I asked.

"Yes I am." she replied.

"But, your resume had the name J. Nitram on it," I said.

"That is my name David. Or did you forget that too?" she asked with a concerned tone of voice.

"No, I didn't forget you. I assumed the initial "J" must have been an abbreviation for some male's name because all the rest of the applications on my desk applying for the Director of Leadership position are men. I'm so embarrassed right now. I apologize for my ignorance!" I said.

I then asked, "Why are you applying for this position?"

She replied, by saying, "For two reasons. First, I was personally asked by your Chief Executive Officer to apply for this position." She paused for a moment.

"What's the second reason why you applied?" I asked.

"Well, the second reason was to…see you again." she slowly replied.

Of course, I had to ask the typical, stupid, naïve question, "Why did you want to see me again?" Again, she paused for a moment to collect her thoughts.

"After I won the Young Leader of Tomorrow Award that afternoon at Leadership Camp, you were the last person to give me a hug and congratulate me. You left a lasting impression with me and I'll never forget what you said to me before we said good-bye," she said with a sincere voice.

I racked my brain as to what she was referring to, but once again I had to humble myself, and asked, "I apologize, but what was it that I said to you?"

She replied, by saying, "You told me that Dr. B. may have taught us the steps of how to become a good leader, but you showed us and involved all of us how to become a good leader. I hope someday I can repay you for what you have showed me, and made me feel these past two weeks. I'm honored to call you my friend and who knows maybe someday you can lead me again professionally!"

"Wow! I said that?" I asked.

"You sure did, so I hope you mean what you said? Do you think I'm qualified for the position?" she asked.

"Absolutely. You have what it takes to be the Director of our new Leadership Department." I said with extreme confidence.

"I only have one more question?" she asked.

"What's that?" I asked.

"It's kind of personal. I hope you don't mind?" she asked. I'm not sure what she was going to ask me, but she did peak my interest.

"Go for it. What's the question?" I asked.

"How come you never called me after Leadership Camp?" she asked.

I was speechless. I didn't know what to say. I was fearful that no matter what my response would be it would not be good enough for her. So, I did what any other good leader would do. I took the first step and...*Looked Fear in the Face* and said, "Jill...I was wrong not to call you after Leadership Camp, so allow me to make it up to you. First, Let me make good on my old promise and offer you the new position! And second, I promise to keep in touch whether you accept the new position or not."

Jill gladly replied, and said, "I'll accept your kind offer. Now, let's see if you can do step two right and *Envision* what's next for me!"

Acknowledgments

This book is dedicated to my wife Jill. She is my inspiration. Her belief in me is how I was able to write this book. Her ability to lead is why I chose her to be the lead character in this book. Jill's quiet leadership style has made me a better husband and father to our son. I cannot thank her enough for everything she does for me. I would also like to thank the following people:

Thank you Lord for sending us Jesus who was and will be the best example of not good leadership but great leadership.

Thank you Mom for raising all five of us by yourself and working three jobs. You were my first example of what a good leader should be and do.

Thank you Robert Wegman, Danny Wegman, and all the managers I have worked for during my career at Wegmans. All of you have molded me into becoming a good leader.

Thank you Steve Chichelli, John Miller, and Ryan Hall for giving me honest feedback. Plus, thanks for allowing me to lead all of you on our Information Technology Project.

Thank you Dr. Berman and all my other M.B.A. professors at St. John Fisher College. All of you taught me academically what Leadership was all about.

About the Author

David Tantillo's credentials with regards to understanding the concept of leadership were earned through hard work academically, professionally, and personally. Academically, David Tantillo holds three different degrees. He earned an Associate in Applied Science in Marketing at Monroe Community College, a Bachelor of Science with a concentration in Finance and a minor in Economics at the State University of New York at Brockport, and a Master's in Business Administration at St. John Fisher College. While at St. John Fisher, David was elected to "Who's Who Among Students in American Universities and Colleges" and earned the St. John Fisher College M.B.A. Scholarly Achievement Award for having the highest cumulative grade point average in his graduating class.

Professionally, David has worked for Wegmans Food Markets for over 23 years with 21 of those years being in a part-time or full-time management position. Wegmans Food Markets was named the #1 company to work for in America according to *Fortune* Magazine in 2005. The company has been in the top 100 companies for eight consecutive years. While at Wegmans, he held other leadership positions like being a Wegmans Scholarship Steering Committee Member, a United Way Account Executive, a United Way Day of Caring Coordinator, a Safety Team Leader, and a mentor for Career, Summer, and Service Management Interns. He also completed 28 company-sponsored seminars, which has helped him in developing young managers; in addition, he also helped teach two of these seminars to several other Wegmans employees. Currently, David is the Project Team Leader of a cutting edge procurement system for the Information Technology Department at Wegmans.

Personally, David has learned how to be a leader inside and outside of his home. He has learned how to be a good servant leader to his wife Jill for the past five years and his son for the past two years. David has captained and/or coached several recreational sports teams the last twenty-five years. Finally, David is an Ordained Elder and is currently part of Session for a Presbyterian Church in Western New York.

Printed in the United States
59415LVS00005B/526-630